EIGHTH-GRADE MATH MINUTES

One Hundred Minutes to Better Basic Skills

Written by
Doug Stoffel

Editor: Jennifer Busby
Cover Illustrator: Rick Grayson
Production: Carlie Hayashi
Cover Designer: Barbara Peterson
Art Director: Moonhee Pak
Managing Editor: Betsy Morris, Ph D

TABLE OF CONTENTS

INTRODUCTION

Eighth grade is an extremely important year in math for students. It is often the final year for students to solidify their basic math skills before moving on to the abstract world of algebra and geometry. The focus of *Eighth-Grade Math Minutes* is math fluency—teaching students to solve problems effortlessly and rapidly. The problems in this book provide students with practice in every key area of eighth-grade math instruction, including:

- computation
- number sense
- graphing
- problem solving
- measurement
- data analysis and probability
- spatial connections
- critical reasoning
- algebra and functions
- geometry

Use this comprehensive resource to improve your students' overall math fluency, which will promote greater self-confidence in their math skills as well as provide the everyday practice necessary to succeed in testing situations.

Eighth-Grade Math Minutes features 100 "Minutes." Each Minute consists of 10 classroom-tested problems of varying degrees of difficulty for students to complete within a one- to two-minute period. This unique format offers students an ongoing opportunity to improve their own fluency in a manageable, nonthreatening format. The quick, timed format, combined with instant feedback, makes this a challenging and motivational assignment students will look forward to using each day. Students become active learners as they discover mathematical relationships and apply acquired understanding to complex situations and to the solution of realistic problems in each Minute.

How to Use This Book

Eighth-Grade Math Minutes is designed to be implemented in numerical order, starting with Minute One. Students who need the most support will find the order in which skills are introduced helpful in building and retaining confidence and success. For example, the first time that students are asked to provide the value of pi to the hundredths place, the digits in the ones and tenths places are provided. The second time, the digit in the ones place is provided. It is not until the third time that students are asked the value of pi that they must recall the number without additional support.

Eighth-Grade Math Minutes can be used in a variety of ways. Use one Minute a day as a warm-up activity, review, assessment, or homework assignment. Other uses include incentive projects and extra credit. Keep in mind that students will get the most benefit from their daily Minute if they receive immediate feedback. If you assign the Minute as homework, correct it in class as soon as students are settled at the beginning of the day.

If you use the Minutes as a timed activity, place the paper facedown on the students' desks or display it as a transparency. Use a clock or kitchen timer to measure one minute—or more if needed. As the Minutes become more advanced, use your discretion on extending the time frame to several minutes if needed. Encourage students to concentrate on completing each problem successfully and not to dwell on problems they cannot complete. At the end of the allotted time, have the students stop working. Then, read the answers from the answer key (pages 108–112) or display them on a transparency. Have students correct their own work and record their scores on the Minute Journal reproducible (page 6). Then, have the class go over each problem together to discuss the solution(s). Spend more time on problems that were clearly challenging for most of the class. Tell students that problems that seemed difficult for them will appear again on future Minutes, and that they will have another opportunity for success.

Teach students strategies for improving their scores, especially if you time their work on each Minute. Include strategies such as

- leave more time-consuming problems for last
- come back to problems they are unsure of after they have completed all other problems
- make educated guesses when they encounter problems with which they are unfamiliar
- rewrite word problems as number problems
- use mental math whenever possible
- underline important information
- draw pictures

Students will ultimately learn to apply these strategies to other timed-test situations.

The Minutes are designed to improve math fluency and should not be included as part of a student's overall math grade. However, the Minutes provide an excellent opportunity for you to see which skills the class as a whole needs to practice or review. This information can help you plan the content of future math lessons. A class that consistently has difficulty with reading graphs, for example, may make excellent use of your lesson in that area, especially if the students know they will have another opportunity to achieve success in reading graphs on a future Minute. Have students file their Math Journal and Minutes for the week in a location accessible to you both. You will find that math skills that require review will be revealed during class discussions of each Minute. You may find it useful to review the week's Minutes again at the end of the week with the class before sending them home with students.

While you will not include student Minute scores in your formal grading, you may wish to recognize improvements by awarding additional privileges or offering a reward if the entire class scores above a certain level for a week or more. Showing students that you recognize their efforts provides additional motivation to succeed.

MINUTE JOURNAL

NAME _____

MINUTE	DATE	SCORE	MINUTE	DATE	SCORE	MINUTE	DATE	SCORE	MINUTE	DATE	SCORE
1			26			51			76		
2			27			52			77		
3			28			53			78		
4			29			54			79		
5			30			55			80		
6			31			56			81		
7			32			57			82		
8			33			58			83		
9			34			59			84		
10			35			60			85		
11			36			61			86		
12			37			62			87		
13			38			63			88		
14			39			64			89		
15			40			65			90		
16			41			66			91		
17			42			67			92		
18			43			68			93		
19			44			69			94		
20			45			70			95		
21			46			71			96		
22			47			72			97		
23			48			73			98		
24			49			74			99		
25			50			75			100		

Eighth-Grade Math Minutes © 2007 Creative Teaching Press

SCOPE AND SEQUENCE

MINUTE 1

1. $2^3 =$

2. $27 \div 9 + 3 =$

3. If $m + 40 = 75$, then $m =$ _____.

4. Number of letters in the alphabet minus the number of months in a year? _____

5. $(4 + 2)^2 =$

6. Write $3 \cdot 3 \cdot 3 \cdot 3$ in exponential form. _____

7. $8 \cdot 9 =$

8. $\dfrac{48}{6} =$

9. $1^{10} =$

10. $5 + (4)(3) =$

BONUS! Farmer Doug has some pigs and chickens.
One day he counted 24 legs and 7 heads in the barnyard.
How many of each animal did Farmer Doug count? _____

Eighth-Grade Math Minutes © 2007 Creative Teaching Press

MINUTE 2

1. $(2)(3)(4) =$

2. Write $4 \cdot 4 \cdot 4 \cdot 4 \cdot 4$ in exponential form. _____

3. $\dfrac{-4}{2} = $ =

4. Bobby thinks that $5^2 = 10$.
What is wrong with this answer? _____

5. $4 + 6 \cdot 2 = 4 + 12$ Circle: True   or   False

6. If $a = 5$ and $b = 6$, then what does ab equal? _____

7. Miss White wants to buy 5 value meals at Mel's Diner.
What is a reasonable total for her purchase?
    a. $25   **b.** $1,000   **c.** $100   **d.** $10

8. 12 snakes have how many eyes altogether? _____

9. $5 + (9)(6) =$

10. Which of these operations should be completed first
when solving an equation?
    a. $\times$ **b.** $+$ **c.** $(\ )$ **d.** $\div$

Eighth-Grade Math Minutes © 2007 Creative Teaching Press

NAME: _____

MINUTE 3

1. $2(5 + 8) =$

2. Rewrite $4 \cdot 4 \cdot 6 \cdot 4 \cdot 4 \cdot 6$ using exponents. _____

3. $\dfrac{3(4 + 2)}{9} =$

4. Brad thinks that $2 \cdot 2 \cdot 2 \cdot 2$ is represented by 4^2.
What is wrong with this answer? _____

5. $3.2 \times 10^3 =$

6. If $a = 2$ and $b = 3$, then what does ab^2 equal? _____

7. $0.043 \times 10^3 =$

8. A mouse has 14 whiskers.
How many whiskers do 3 mice have? _____

9. $5 + (9)(6) - 4 =$

10. Which of these operations should be completed
<u>last</u> when solving an equation?

     a. $\times$ **b.** $+$ **c.** $(\ )$ **d.** $\div$

Eighth-Grade Math Minutes © 2007 Creative Teaching Press

MINUTE 4

1. $3.57 \times 10^3 =$

2. $2^2 \cdot 2^3 =$

3. Which of these represents a whole number?
Circle all that apply.

    a. 4   **b.** 3.2   **c.** $\dfrac{3}{4}$ **d.** $\dfrac{3}{4}$

4. Which of these represents an integer?
Circle all that apply.

    a. −3   **b.** 4   **c.** $\dfrac{8}{10}$ **d.** 6.2

5. Which expression is correctly written in scientific notation?

    a. 398×10^1 **b.** $\overline{4}$

    c. 3.98×10^4 **d.** $.398 \times 10^3$

6. $\dfrac{8 + 4 \cdot 3}{5} =$

7. $2^{-2} =$

8. $\dfrac{3^3}{3^2} =$

9. $\sqrt{25} =$

10. $3(4^2 + 1) =$

MINUTE 5

1. $3^2 \cdot 3 \cdot 3 \cdot 3 = 3^4$ Circle: True   or   False

2. Write 5,806 in scientific notation. _____

3. $2^{-3} = \dfrac{1}{2^3}$ Circle: True   or   False

4. $\sqrt{64} =$

5. $3[8 + (4 + 2)] =$

6. What does a equal in this problem? $8 = 2^a$ _____

7. $x \cdot x \cdot x =$

8. If $a = 6$ and $b = 2$, then what does a^b equal? _____

9. $\dfrac{2^5}{2^3} =$

10. According to the graph, which of these is true?
    a. The later in the day it is, the hotter it is.
    b. Temperature goes up and then down during the day.
    c. Temperature is always lowest in the evening.
    d. Temperature decreases when it rains.

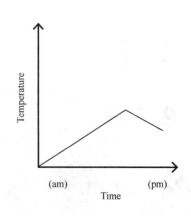

Eighth-Grade Math Minutes © 2007 Creative Teaching Press

MINUTE 6

1. $2\sqrt{49} =$

2. Write 20,136 in scientific notation. _____

3. $\left(\dfrac{2}{3}\right)^2 =$

4. $2^2 \cdot 2^2 = 2^4$ Circle: True   or   False

5. $\dfrac{2 \cdot 3 \cdot 4}{2 \cdot 3} =$

6. $\sqrt{16} \cdot \sqrt{25} =$

7. According to the graph on the right,
   would it be a good idea to invest in this company?
        Circle: Yes   or   No

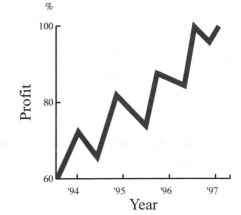

8. $[(2 + 3) \cdot 4] =$

9. $\dfrac{4^6}{4^4} =$

10. $3^{-2} =$

BONUS!

The sum of two numbers is 9 and their difference is 3.
What is their product? _____

MINUTE 7

1. Circle the numbers that are integers:

   5   − 4   2.6 $0.\overline{8}$ 100

2. Round 0.682 to the nearest tenth. _____

3. Is $\sqrt{60}$ closer to 3 or 4? _____

4. $\left(\sqrt{4}\right)^2 =$

5. Which of these operations should be completed first?

   a. ÷   **b.** −   **c.** ( )   **d.** exponents

6. If 6 out of 30 people over the age of 100 are male, how many are female? _____

7. Janet's dinner costs $7.50. If she wants to leave a 10% tip, how much extra should she leave? _____

8. Wally completed 7 out of 10 baskets. What percent is this? _____

9. $6(0.4 + 0.3) =$

10. $4 \cdot 5 \cdot 6 \cdot 2 \cdot 0 \cdot 11 =$

MINUTE 8

1. $3.064 \times 1,000 =$

2. Rewrite $4 \cdot 4 \cdot 4 \cdot 8 \cdot 8 \cdot 4$ using exponents. _____

3. $(4 + 3)(2 + 6) =$

4. $2(8 - 5)^2 =$

5. Write 26,373 in scientific notation. _____

6. Which of the following is equal to $4^8 \cdot 4^4$?
   a. 4^2 **b.** 4^{32} **c.** 4^4 **d.** 4^{12}

7. $\dfrac{23}{50} =$ _____ %

8. Beth needs to add a 10% tip to her $12 meal.
How much money does she need to add? _____

9. $0.063 \times 100 =$

10. If $a = 3$ and $b = 4$, then $b^a =$ _____.

MINUTE 9

1. Is $\sqrt{8}$ closer to 2 or 3? _____

2. $8^{-2} =$

3. $\dfrac{7^8}{7^6} =$

4. $4.068 \times 10^2 =$

5. $46.8 \times 10^{-2} =$

6. $2(2 \cdot 2)^2 =$

7. If $a = 2$ and $b = 3$, then does $ab = ba$?   Circle: Yes   or   No

8. Correctly write 36.2×10^3 in scientific notation. _____

9. $\dfrac{12}{25} =$ _____ %

10. $7\left(\dfrac{1}{2} + \dfrac{1}{2}\right) =$

BONUS! What is the sum of the first 5 prime numbers? _____

Eighth-Grade Math Minutes © 2007 Creative Teaching Press

MINUTE 10

1. The Gigantosaurus weighs 2.3×10^4 pounds.
   How many pounds is this? _____

2. $4(0.6 + 0.6) =$

3. Write 0.0059 in scientific notation. _____

4. Rewrite $a \cdot a \cdot b \cdot c \cdot a \cdot b$ using exponents. _____

5. $\dfrac{7}{20} =$ _____ %

6. $\dfrac{8^8}{8^3} =$

7. $(8 - 6)^{-2} =$

8. $24 = 2^3 \cdot 3$ Circle: True   or   False

9. If $a = 10$ and $b = 2$, then $\dfrac{a}{b} \cdot b =$ _____.

10. All of the following mean to multiply except:

    a. $6x$ **b.** $6(x)$ **c.** $\dfrac{x}{6}$ **d.** $(6)(x)$

MINUTE 11

1. Order the integers {–10, –25, 25, 10, –50} from least to greatest. _____

2. $\dfrac{9^5}{9^3} =$

15 in.

3. What is the area of the rectangle? _____   10 in.

4. $-2 \cdot -3 =$

5. $-9(4 + 2 + 3) =$

6. $-2 + -3 =$

7. $\dfrac{48}{200} =$ _____ %

Use > , < , or = to complete Problems 8–10.

8. 3 _____ –6

9. –5 _____ –3

10. 0 _____ –8

BONUS! Use the numbers 1, 2, 3, and 4 to fill in the boxes to make the equation true.

$$\boxed{} \times \boxed{} + \boxed{} - \boxed{} = 10$$

Eighth-Grade Math Minutes © 2007 Creative Teaching Press

MINUTE 12

1. $-8(-7) =$

2. $-8 + 7 =$

3. Order from greatest to least: 12, -4, 8, -3, 0. _____

4. $-8(3^2 + 1) =$

5. Write 843 in scientific notation. _____

6. Find the volume of the box. _____

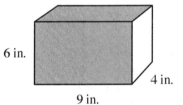

6 in.

9 in.

4 in.

7. $(-6)^2 =$

8. $20 = 2^2 \cdot 5$ Circle: True   or   False

9. $2\left(\sqrt{81}\right) =$

10. $\sqrt{16} \cdot \sqrt{36} =$

BONUS!   Complete the sequence: 1, 1, 2, 3, 5, ____, ____, ____.

MINUTE 13

1. $5^2 = (-5)^2$ Circle: True   or   False

2. If $2x - 7 = 19$, then $x =$ _____ .

3. $(-2)(-3)(4) =$

4. $\sqrt{(2 \cdot 5 \cdot 10)} =$

5. $\left(\dfrac{1}{3}\right)^2 =$

6. $-10 + (-12) =$

7. $10 + (-12) =$

Use = 5, = –3, and = –2 to complete Problems 8–10.

8. $ab =$

9. $b + c =$

10. $a^c =$

BONUS! Find the next row of numbers in Pascal's triangle.

```
            1
          1   1
        1   2   1
      1   3   3   1
    1   4   6   4   1
```

Eighth-Grade Math Minutes © 2007 Creative Teaching Press

MINUTE 14

1. $|-5| =$

2. Michaela says that $|3|$ is bigger than $|-8|$.
    Is Michaela's statement true or false? _____

3. Write 1,407 in scientific notation. _____

4. $3\sqrt{9} =$

5. Order the numbers from least to greatest: $-10, 20, |-11|, 0.$ _____

6. 134 minutes = _____ hours + _____ minutes

7. If $a = \dfrac{-10}{5}$, then $a =$ _____.

8. $(-7)^2 =$

9. $\dfrac{4^{10}}{4^4} =$

10. A negative $(-)$ times a positive $(+)$ equals a _____.
    Circle: positive   or   negative

Eighth-Grade Math Minutes © 2007 Creative Teaching Press

MINUTE 15

1. $10 - |-5| =$

2. $4(3 - 8) =$

3. $12 - 20 =$

4. $\sqrt{4} \cdot \sqrt{100} =$

5. $\dfrac{(-8)(-2)}{-8} =$

6. Based on the number line, which numbers are identified?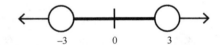
   a. All numbers bigger than –3 and smaller than 3
   b. All numbers between –3 and 3 including –3 and 3
   c. All numbers bigger than 0
   d. All numbers less than 3

7. $-3 > -5$ Circle: True or False

8. A negative (–) divided by a negative (–) equals a _____.

9. $6^2 = (-6)^2$ Circle: True or False

10. Complete the table on the right by finding x.

1	2	3	4	5
1	4	9	16	x

Eighth-Grade Math Minutes © 2007 Creative Teaching Press

MINUTE 16

1. $|-10| + |-8| =$

2. $(-3) + (-4) =$

3. Based on the number line, which numbers are identified?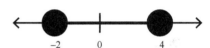
   a. All numbers bigger than –2
   b. All numbers between –2 and 4 including –2 and 4
   c. All numbers bigger than 0
   d. All numbers less than 4

4. $(-) \cdot (-) \cdot (-) =$
   a. +   **b.** –   **c.** 0

5. $-(4^2) =$

6. $-50 + 20 =$

7. If $a = -8$, then $4a =$ _____.

8. If $g = \dfrac{-8}{4}$ then $g =$ _____.

9. A negative (–) plus a negative (–) equals a negative (–).
   Circle: True   or   False

10. Is $\dfrac{8}{10}$ an integer?   Circle: Yes   or   No

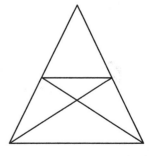

BONUS! How many total triangles are in the picture? _____

MINUTE 17

1. Which of these is not equal to $\frac{1}{4}$?   Circle: $\frac{2}{4}$, $\frac{4}{16}$, 25%, 0.25, $\frac{5}{20}$

2. If $x = -5 + 3 - 3$, then $x =$ _____ .

3. $\left|\dfrac{-8}{4}\right| =$

4. Which of these is the greatest number?

    a. $\dfrac{4}{5}$ **b.** -3 **c.** $\left|-8\right|$ **d.** 4

5. $-12 + (-5) =$

6. Which value of a would make $a - 5 > -1$ true?

    a. 2 **b.** -2 **c.** 3 **d.** 6

7. $-12 \cdot -5 =$

8. $27 = 3 \cdot 3^3$ Circle: True or False

9. $\dfrac{(-)}{(+)} = (-)$ Circle: True or False

10. $\dfrac{14 \cdot 13 \cdot (-12)}{14 \cdot 13 \cdot 4} =$

Eighth-Grade Math Minutes © 2007 Creative Teaching Press

MINUTE 18

1. $18 + (-16) =$

2. $18 \div -3 =$

3. $(-5)(6)(-7) =$

4. On Monday Luke's business lost $15.
On Tuesday it made $8. On Wednesday it broke even.
What is the total profit or loss during those 3 days? _____

5. $\dfrac{8}{12} + \dfrac{3}{12} =$

6. $\left(\dfrac{-1}{4}\right)\left(\dfrac{1}{3}\right) =$

7. $2^2 \cdot 3^2 = 36$ Circle: True   or   False

8. $-5 \cdot \sqrt{16} =$

9. $(-2)(-3) + (-4)(-2) =$

10. If $a^2 > 20$, then which of the following could be a value of a? *Circle all that apply.*
    a. 6   **b.** 3   **c.** (−8)   **d.** 2

BONUS!
Bees are leaving their hive at a rate of 10 per hour, and they are reentering the hive at a rate of 6 per hour. If the hive starts with 100 bees, how long will it take before the hive is empty? _____

MINUTE 19

1. $0.08 + 0.3 =$

2. $-2 \cdot |-11| =$

3. $\left(\sqrt{25}\right)^2 =$

4. If $4x - 3 = 25$, then $x =$ _____.

5. $4.38 \times 10^3 =$

6. Write $3 \cdot 3 \cdot 4 \cdot 4 \cdot 3 \cdot 4$ using exponents. _____

7. $4 + (-2)(3) =$

8. Is it possible for 15% of $25 to be $375?   Circle: Yes   or   No

9. $-6 + -5 =$

10. Which value of n will make $2n > 8$ true?
     a. 3   **b.** 4   **c.** 5   **d.** −10

BONUS!
Kyle mows 4 lawns a day, 4 days a week, 4 weeks
a month, and 4 months a year. He makes $25 per lawn.
How much money did he make last year? _____

Eighth-Grade Math Minutes © 2007 Creative Teaching Press

MINUTE 20

1. $(-0.6) + 0.8 =$

2. $-14 - (2)(3) =$

3. $8 - (-3) =$

4. $\left(7 + \sqrt{9}\right)^2 =$

5. If $2a + 3 < 10$, then which of these could be a value of a?

    a. 6   **b.** 4   **c.** 2   **d.** 10

6. Write 36% as a decimal. _____

7. How would you find 28% of 612?

    a. Take 0.28 multiplied by 612

    b. Take 0.28 divided by 612

    c. Take 0.0028 multiplied by 612

    d. Take 0.028 divided by 612

8. If $y = x^2$ and $x = (-8)$, then $y =$ _____.

9. $3|-10| =$

10. $P = 2L + 2W$. Find P if $L = 10$ and $W = 5$. _____

Eighth-Grade Math Minutes © 2007 Creative Teaching Press

NAME: _____

MINUTE 21

1. Find 16% of 83. _____

2. $3 - \left(-\dfrac{8}{2}\right) =$

3. Michelle got 23 out of 30 questions correct on her quiz.
   To find what her percent correct is, Michelle should:
   a. Take 30 divided by 23 and then multiply by 100
   b. Take 23 divided by 30 and then multiply by 100
   c. Take 23 multiplied by 30 and then multiply by 100
   d. Take 30 multiplied by 23 and then multiply by 100

4. Rewrite $\dfrac{1}{10}$ as a decimal. _____

5. $\left(\dfrac{-2}{3}\right)\left(\dfrac{-1}{5}\right) =$

6. Is $0.\overline{6}$ a rational or an irrational number? _____

7. Write 0.0382 in scientific notation. _____

8. $\dfrac{6(-8)}{-4} =$

9. $\dfrac{8^{11}}{8^{9}} =$

10. $3 + (-3)^2 =$

Eighth-Grade Math Minutes © 2007 Creative Teaching Press

MINUTE 22

1. Write 16% as a decimal and a fraction. _____

2. $\left(\sqrt{16} + |-2|\right)^2 =$

3. What percent is $\dfrac{3}{4}$? _____

4. How would you find out what $\dfrac{1}{25}$ is as a decimal using a calculator?

     a. Punch in "1 divided by 11"   **b.** Punch in "11 divided by 1"

     c. Punch in "1 times 11"   **d.** Punch in "11 times 1"

5. If $-48 = 6(a)$, then $a =$ _____.

6. Find 10% of 25. _____

7. Write the equation to find 12% of 84. _____

Use >, <, or = to complete Problems 8–10.

8. 0.05 _____ 50%

9. 57.8% _____ 0.578

10. $\dfrac{4}{5}$ _____ 0.21

MINUTE 23

1. Find 15% of $20. _____

2. If $\dfrac{12}{20} = \dfrac{x}{100}$, then $x =$ _____.

3. Is it possible for 20% of 45 to be 9?   Circle: Yes   or   No

4. What is $\dfrac{3}{4}$ of $\dfrac{1}{2}$? _____

5. Circle all answers that are equal to 60%.

   a. $\dfrac{3}{4}$ **b.** 0.6   **c.** $\dfrac{8}{10}$ **d.** 0.06

6. If Mark gets 41 out of 55 questions right on a test,
   what equation would he use to determine the percent correct? _____

7. Circle the answer that does not belong:

   a. 0.55   **b.** $\dfrac{11}{20}$ **c.** 55%   **d.** $\dfrac{1}{25}$

8. If $\dfrac{1}{2} - \dfrac{1}{3} = x$, then $x =$ _____.

9. Three subtracted from a number is 12. What is the number? _____

10. Write $a \cdot a \cdot b \cdot a \cdot b \cdot b \cdot b$ using exponents. _____

Eighth-Grade Math Minutes © 2007 Creative Teaching Press

MINUTE 24

1. $\frac{3}{4}$ of 25 =

2. Three times a number is –18. What is the number? _____

3. Find the perimeter of the regular hexagon. _____

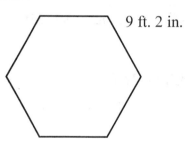

9 ft. 2 in.

4. 20% of 35 =

5. Circle all answers that are equal to 80%.

    a. 0.8   **b.** $\frac{4}{5}$ **c.** 0.08   **d.** $\frac{8}{10}$

6. Simplify: $b^2 \cdot b \cdot b =$

7. Which of the following is the greatest number?

    a. $\frac{1}{2}$ **b.** 65%   **c.** 0.55   **d.** 0.60

8. Evelynn goes to a restaurant and her bill is $12.
She wants to leave a 15% tip. How much should she leave for the tip? _____

9. What percent is $\frac{3}{4}$? _____

10. $4 \cdot |-8| =$

MINUTE 25

1. 50% of 200 =

2. A number divided by –3 is –5. What is the number?_____

3. Original price: $10   New price: $7   Circle: Discount   or   Mark Up

4. To find sales tax, multiply the cost of an item by 0.05.
   Circle: True   or   False

5. Circle the answers that are equal to 8%.

   a. 8   **b.** 0.08   **c.** $\frac{1}{10}$ **d.** $\frac{8}{10}$

6. Emily puts $100 in the bank and earns 4% interest per year.
   How much interest will she earn in one year? _____

7. Which answer does not belong?

   a. 0.1   **b.** 10%   **c.** $\frac{1}{10}$ **d.** 0.001

8. Circle which answer is greater: 10% of 500   or   20% of 400

9. $4(\sqrt{100}) =$

10. $6^{-2} =$

BONUS!
Grampy Wolf has 7 coins in his pocket worth 65 cents.
   How many quarters, dimes, and nickels does he have? _____

Eighth-Grade Math Minutes © 2007 Creative Teaching Press

MINUTE 26

1. $\dfrac{3}{4} \cdot \dfrac{3}{5} =$

2. $10.05 = 10\dfrac{1}{2}$ Circle: True   or   False

3. Circle the answer that is greater: 20% of 400   or   25% of 500

4. Order from least to greatest: $\dfrac{4}{5}$, $\dfrac{1}{10}$, 25%, 0.05. _____

5. $-\dfrac{3}{4} = \dfrac{-3}{4}$ Circle: True   or   False

6. $\left(\dfrac{-2}{3}\right)\left(\dfrac{2}{3}\right) =$

7. The reciprocal of $\dfrac{1}{10}$ is _____.

8. Reduce: $\dfrac{-8}{24} =$

9. Find the mean temperature in Eagletown for the past 5 days. _____

Mon.	Tues.	Wed.	Thurs.	Fri.
60°	80°	65°	75°	70°

10. Write $\dfrac{4}{5}$ as a mixed number. _____

MINUTE 27

1. $\dfrac{3}{8} \cdot \dfrac{4}{5} =$

2. $10.75 = 10\dfrac{3}{4}$ Circle: True   or   False

3. Order from least to greatest: $\dfrac{4}{5}$, 0.78, 15%, $\dfrac{1}{25}$. _____

4. $-\dfrac{3}{4} = \dfrac{(-3)}{4}$ Circle: True   or   False

5. The reciprocal of $\dfrac{1}{25}$ is _____.

6. Reduce: $\dfrac{-8}{40} =$

7. $\dfrac{5}{11} \cdot \dfrac{-11}{6} =$

8. Write $10\dfrac{3}{4}$ as an improper fraction. _____

9. Circle the answer that is greater: 25% of 400   or   20% of 1,000

10. Which of these are prime numbers? *Circle all that apply.*

     5   7   12   8   11   2   20   45

Eighth-Grade Math Minutes © 2007 Creative Teaching Press

MINUTE 28

1. When dividing two fractions, you must flip the _____ fraction over and then multiply.

2. When multiplying fractions such as $\frac{3}{6} \cdot \frac{2}{8}$ how can the fractions be reduced? *Circle all that apply.*

    a. Up and down   **b.** Diagonally

    c. Both numbers on the top   **d.** Both numbers on the bottom

3. Circle the answer that does not belong:

    $\frac{3}{4}$ $\left| -\frac{3}{4} \right|$ 0.75   0.075   75%

4. Compare using > or <: $x \bigcirc y$, if $\frac{x}{y} = 0.3$ and both x and y are positive numbers. _____

5. Which of the following operations always produce a positive answer?

    a. A negative times a negative   **b.** A negative divided by a negative

    c. A negative plus a negative   **d.** A negative minus a negative

6. What is one-third of one-half? _____

7. The distance around the earth (circumference) is 4.0074×10^9 centimeters. Write this in decimal form. _____

8. Is p a rational or irrational number? _____

Insert parenthesis ( ) to make the equation true for Problems 9–10.

9. $5 - 8 + 2 = -5$

10. $ \widetilde{}\, 3$

MINUTE 29

1. $\dfrac{1}{2} \div \dfrac{3}{4} = \dfrac{1}{2} \cdot \dfrac{4}{3}$ Circle: True   or   False

2. $-8 \cdot -2 + (-3) \cdot 3 =$

3. Write $-2\dfrac{3}{8}$ as an improper fraction. _____

4. Write 4,332 in scientific notation. _____

5. Original price: $100   New price: $68   What is the percent of decrease? _____

6. Which one does not belong?

   $\dfrac{4}{5}$ 25%   0.25 $\left|-\dfrac{1}{4}\right|$ 0.025

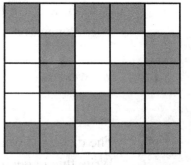

7. What percent of the squares are shaded? _____

8. Which value for x will solve this equation: $\dfrac{x}{4} + 2 = 8$?

   a. 32   **b.** 16   **c.** 20   **d.** 24

9. What is $\dfrac{1}{2}$ of $\dfrac{4}{5}$? _____

10. If you multiply 3 negative fractions together, your answer will be _____.
    Circle: positive   or   negative

Eighth-Grade Math Minutes © 2007 Creative Teaching Press

MINUTE 30

1. To divide fractions, flip the first fraction over and then multiply.
   Circle: True   or   False

2. $-4(3^2 - 2) =$

3. The reciprocal of $3\frac{1}{4}$ is _____ .

4. A whole number is a(n) _____ number.
   Circle: rational   or   irrational

5. Write $-12\frac{2}{3}$ as an improper fraction. _____

6. What is the tax on a $50 pair of shoes if the tax rate is 6%? _____

7. $\dfrac{-10 - 9 - 5}{-8} =$

8. $\dfrac{4}{5}$ of 80 =

9. $10^{-2} =$

10. Find the area of the hexagon.

12
7   4
10

IN		F		OUT
4		U		7
7		N		13
5	$\rightarrow$	C	$\rightarrow$	9
3		T		5
10		I		19
3		O		5
15		N		?

BONUS! What is the missing number? _____

MINUTE 31

1. To divide fractions, multiply the first fraction by the reciprocal of the second fraction.

    Circle: True   or   False

2. $3 \cdot -3 + 3 \cdot -3 =$

3. The reciprocal of $3\frac{1}{4}$ is _____.

4. Complete the table on the right.

Fraction	Decimal	Percent
$\frac{5}{20}$		

5. Write $-4\frac{2}{5}$ as an improper fraction. _____

6. $\frac{-3}{5} + \frac{4}{5} =$

7. $\left(\frac{-2}{5}\right)^2 =$

8. $\frac{4}{5}$ of $16 =$

9. $\frac{-3}{8} + \frac{-2}{8} =$

10. If $\frac{3}{5} = \frac{a}{20}$, then $a =$ _____.

BONUS! If a square has an area of 64 square inches what is the perimeter? _____

Eighth-Grade Math Minutes © 2007 Creative Teaching Press

MINUTE 32

1. Find the lowest common denominator of $\frac{1}{3}$ and $\frac{2}{5}$. _____

2. $\frac{2}{9} + \frac{3}{9} = $ =

3. $\frac{-5}{7} \cdot \frac{7}{8} = $

4. $\frac{1}{2}(-5 + 9) = $

5. Write 0.0084 in scientific notation. _____

6. What is 10% of 900? _____

7. $20^{-2} = $

8. $(-5)(6)(-2) = $

9. $18 \div -3 = $

10. The diameter of a tire is 20 inches. Which of these is a good estimate for the distance around the tire?
    Hint: $C = \pi d$

    a. 60 inches   **b.** 80 inches   **c.** 100 inches   **d.** 40 inches

MINUTE 33

1. $7(-3)2 =$

2. What does the *a* equal in this problem: $27 = 3^a$? _____

3. $\sqrt{36} =$

4. $\left(\dfrac{1}{8}\right)^2 =$

5. Is $\sqrt{49}$ closer to 5 or 6? _____

6. On five different tests Jake got: 75, 80, 81, 96, and 100.
   Which of the following would be greater? Circle: the answer below.
   Jake's median score   or   Jake's mean score

7. $\dfrac{3}{25} =$ ____%

8. $\dfrac{-12}{-4} =$

9. Reduce: $-13\dfrac{24}{40} =$

10. $|-8| \cdot |-9| =$

Eighth-Grade Math Minutes © 2007 Creative Teaching Press

MINUTE 34

1. Complete the table on the right.

Fraction	Decimal	Percent
		36%

2. If $3a - 7 > 14$, then which of these could a be?

    a. 8   **b.** 5   **c.** 1   **d.** −8

3. If $y = x^3$ and $x = -3$, then what does y equal? _____

4. $-\sqrt{6} =$

5. $\left(\sqrt{16}\right)^2 =$

6. $\left(\dfrac{-1}{4}\right)\left(\dfrac{-3}{5}\right) =$

7. $10 + (-6)(-7) - 1 =$

8. $\dfrac{12^3}{12^5} =$

9. Find x if $\dfrac{4x}{5} = 20$. $x =$ _____

10. In the problem $y = 2x + 3$, find y if $x = 4$. $y =$ _____

Eighth-Grade Math Minutes © 2007 Creative Teaching Press

MINUTE 35

1. Order from greatest to least: $-21, 11, 0, -5, -4\frac{2}{5}$. _____

2. Write 0.0000042 in scientific notation. _____

3. $-8 + 6 + (-2) =$

4. $-3|-3| =$

5. What is $\frac{}{14.6}$ as a percent? _____

6. What is $\frac{}{14.6}$ reduced? _____

7. What is $\frac{}{14.6}$ as a decimal? _____

8. What is the reciprocal of $\frac{}{14.6}$? _____

9. Simplify: $7^5 \cdot 7^7 =$

10. When you multiply numbers with the same base, as in problem 9, you _____ exponents.

   a. add   **b.** subtract   **c.** multiply   **d.** divide

BONUS!
Annie's ant population doubles every week. After 3 weeks of doubling, how many ants will she have if her colony started with 50? _____

Eighth-Grade Math Minutes © 2007 Creative Teaching Press

MINUTE 36

1. Order from greatest to least: $-12, -15, -7, 0$. _____

2. Write 34,322 in scientific notation. _____

3. $-8 + (-6) + (-2) =$

4. $5\left|-3+(-7)\right| =$

5. Write $-2\dfrac{3}{11}$ as an improper fraction. _____

6. What is the reciprocal of $\dfrac{?}{14.6}$ _____

7. Simplify: $\dfrac{2 \cdot}{2} =$

8. When you divide numbers with the same base, as in problem 7, you _____ exponents.

    a. add   **b.** subtract   **c.** multiply   **d.** divide

9. Complete the table on the right.

Fraction	Decimal	Percent
	0.3	

10. Solve for f if $\dfrac{f-5}{6} = 4$. _____

Eighth-Grade Math Minutes © 2007 Creative Teaching Press

MINUTE 37

1. Find the lowest common denominator of $\frac{1}{2}$ and $4\frac{1}{3}$. _____

2. $\left(\sqrt{3111}\right)^2 =$

3. $-3 \cdot -6 \cdot -2 =$

4. What is the reciprocal of $3\frac{1}{4}$? _____

5. According to the graph, who has the most points? _____

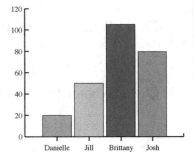

6. Brittany has twice as many points as _____.

7. Round Danielle's score to the nearest 10. _____

8. Write as an improper fraction: $-12\frac{2}{3} =$

9. Simplify: $\frac{2 \cdot ?}{2 \cdot} =$

10. $\frac{-3}{11} + \frac{-4}{11} =$

BONUS!
A number has 5 added to it and is then multiplied by 20. The final answer is 180. What is the original number? _____

Eighth-Grade Math Minutes © 2007 Creative Teaching Press

MINUTE 38

1. Circle the mistake in the problem: $\dfrac{1}{3} + \dfrac{3}{4} = \dfrac{3}{12} + \dfrac{9}{12} = \dfrac{12}{12} = 1$

Use the circle graph to complete Problems 2–4.

Math Points

2. According to the graph, about what percent of the points does Angie have? _____

3. Nicole and Caitlin together have about _____ percent of the points.

4. Which two people represent the largest percent of points earned? _____

Legend:
- ■ Angie
- ▨ Alicia
- □ Chelsey
- ▨ Caitlin
- ▤ Nicole

5. $(-2)^3 = (-2)(-2)(-2) = 8$ Circle: True   or   False

6. $\dfrac{1}{8} \cdot \dfrac{1}{7} =$

7. Find the lowest common denominator of $5\dfrac{1}{2}$ and $\dfrac{3}{7}$. _____

Use the line graph to complete Problems 8–10.

John's Points This Week

8. According to the graph, on which day of the week did John earn the most points? _____

9. About how many points did he earn on Monday? _____

10. Altogether, John earned about how many points this week?
   a. 50–80   **b.** 80–110   **c.** 110–140   **d.** 140–170

Eighth-Grade Math Minutes © 2007 Creative Teaching Press

MINUTE 39

1. Circle the mistake in the problem: $\dfrac{1}{3} - \dfrac{1}{7} = \dfrac{4}{21} - \dfrac{3}{21} = \dfrac{1}{21}$

2. Find the mean: 1, 4, 4, 6, 10. _____

3. What is the mode in Problem 2? _____

4. What is the median in Problem 2? _____

Use the graph to complete Problems 5–8.

5. Which two people have the most points? _____

6. Is there a mode for the graph?
   Circle: Yes   or   No

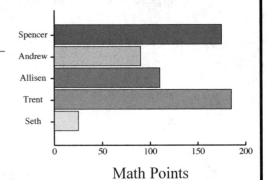

Math Points

7. Which student has the median score? _____

8. Trent has about twice as many points as _____.

9. $-3(2^2 + 1) =$

10. If $a = -2$, then $(3a)^2 =$ _____.

MINUTE 40

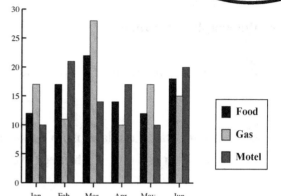

Use the graph to complete Problems 1–3.

1. In which month did Aaron spend the most money? _____

2. In January, did Aaron spend more on food or motel costs? _____

3. How much money was spent on food in June? _____

Use the chart to complete Problems 4–7.

4	3	1	3
2	3	5	✕

4. What is the mode? _____

5. What is the mean? _____

6. What is the median? _____

7. What is the range? _____

8. $5 + 8 \cdot -3 =$

9. $7^{-2} =$

10. $a^{-2} =$

BONUS!
What number (n) must be inserted into the number $3n,85n$ for it to be divisible by 6? _____

MINUTE 41

Use the graph to complete Problems 1–4.

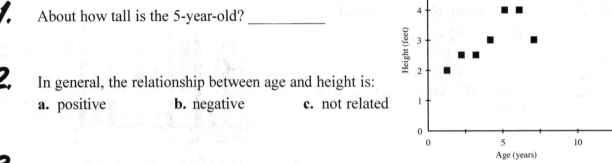

1. About how tall is the 5-year-old? _____

2. In general, the relationship between age and height is:
   a. positive   **b.** negative   **c.** not related

3. How tall is the tallest child in this survey? _____

4. How old is the oldest child in this survey? _____

5. If $\frac{m}{7} = 42$, then $m =$ _____.

6. If $4(x + 2) = 36$, then $x =$ _____.

7. If $r = 20$ and $t = 4$, find d if $d = rt$. $d =$ _____

8. If $\sqrt{x} = 8$, then $x =$ _____.

9. 21 yards = _____ feet

10. 2.5 feet = _____ inches

Eighth-Grade Math Minutes © 2007 Creative Teaching Press

MINUTE 42

Use the graphs to complete Problems 1–4.

Graph A   **Graph B**

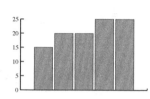
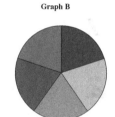

1. Which graph is a circle graph? _____

2. Which graph is a bar graph? _____

Graph C   **Graph D**

3. What graph is a scatter plot? _____

4. Which graph is a line graph? _____

5. Is it possible to have more than one mode for the same set of data?
    Circle: Yes   or   No

6. Is it possible to have more than one mean for the same set of data?
    Circle: Yes   or   No

7. The _____ is the sum of the data divided by the number of pieces of data.

8. In the equation $y = -2x - 3$, find x if $y = 5$. _____

9. Write $-2\frac{3}{8}$ as an improper fraction. _____

10. Seven more than three times a number is 25. What is the number? _____

Eighth-Grade Math Minutes © 2007 Creative Teaching Press

MINUTE 43

1. If $\dfrac{2}{10} = \dfrac{1}{a}$, then $a =$ _____.

2. What is the perimeter of the rectangle? _____

4 cm

8 cm

3. To find the perimeter of a shape, you _____ all the sides together.
   a. add   **b.** subtract   **c.** multiply   **d.** divide

4. Which analogy is similar to <u>Carpet : Area</u>?
   a. Roof : Perimeter   **b.** Yard : Perimeter
   c. Wrapping Paper : Perimeter   **d.** Fence : Perimeter

5. What is the probability of rolling a 5 on a six-sided number cube? _____

6. What is the probability of rolling an even number on a number cube? _____

7. What is the perimeter of a rectangle with a length of 6 and a width of 5? _____

8. $\dfrac{-3}{7} + \dfrac{-3}{7} =$

Use the following information to complete Problems 9–10.
If a computer were to pick a letter at random from the word *mathematics*,
what is the probability that it would choose:

9. the letter *s*? _____

10. the letter *m*? _____

Eighth-Grade Math Minutes © 2007 Creative Teaching Press

MINUTE 44

1. If $\dfrac{3}{5} = \dfrac{24}{a}$, then $a =$ _____.

2. What is the perimeter of the rectangle? _____

4.5 cm

7 cm

3. To find the area of a rectangle, you _____ the length by the width.

    a. add   **b.** subtract   **c.** multiply   **d.** divide

4. Which analogy is similar to <u>Fence : Perimeter</u>?

    a. Carpet : Area   **b.** Tree : Area

    c. Bucket : Area   **d.** Feet : Area

5. What are the prime numbers on a six-sided number cube? _____

6. What is the probability of rolling a prime number
with one roll on a six-sided number cube? _____

7. What is the perimeter of a square with a side length of 2.6? _____

8. $\dfrac{-3}{7} \cdot \dfrac{-3}{7} =$

Use the following information to complete Problems 9–10.
If a computer were to pick a letter at random from the word *geometry*,
what is the probability that it would choose:

9. the letter *y*? _____

10. the letter *e*? _____

MINUTE 45

1. Find the answer for *x* that makes this number sentence true: $2x + 9 > 11$.

    a. 0   **b.** −5   **c.** 10   **d.** −8

2. What is the perimeter of an octagon if each side is 7 inches in length? _____

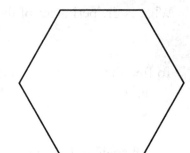

3. Which of these could be the area of a shape?

    a. 25 m   **b.** 10 ft.^{3} **c.** 7 ft.^{2}

4. Which of these could be the perimeter of a shape?

    a. 25 m   **b.** 10 ft.^{3} **c.** 7 ft.^{2}

5. Circle the prime numbers: 5   7   10   11   13

6. What is the perimeter of an equilateral triangle with a side length of 5.5 ft.? _____

7. Complete the sequence: 1, 3, 6, 10, 15, _____, _____, _____

8. $\dfrac{-3}{7} \div \dfrac{-3}{7} =$

Use the following information to complete Problems 9–10.

If a computer were to pick a letter at random from the word *perimeter*, what is the probability that it would choose:

9. the letter *e*? _____

10. a vowel? _____

Eighth-Grade Math Minutes © 2007 Creative Teaching Press

NAME:

MINUTE 46

1. What is the perimeter of the parallelogram? _____

2 ft.

3 in.

2. Which of the following does not produce a negative answer?
   a. A negative times a negative
   b. A negative divided by a positive
   c. A negative plus a negative
   d. A negative times a positive

3. If the radius of a circle is 4.25 feet, what is the diameter? _____

4. A recipe that feeds 6 people calls for 3 cups of flour. Jed is making the recipe for 3 people. How many cups of flour should Jed use? _____

5. Write $\frac{1}{25}$ using exponents. _____

6. Reduce: $\dfrac{a \cdot a \cdot a \cdot b \cdot b}{a \cdot a \cdot b} =$

7. 25% off of $200 is $10.   Circle: True   or   False

8. A room measures 12 feet by 10 feet. Four square yards of carpet have been ordered to cover the floor. Has enough carpet been ordered?
   Circle: Yes   or   No

9. If $x = -5$ and $y = 2x^2$, then $y =$ _____ .

10. $\sqrt{20^2} =$

  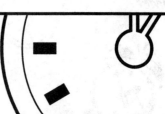

MINUTE 47

1. What is the perimeter of this shape in inches? _____

    1 ft.

    8 in.

2. If the radius of a circle is $4\frac{4}{5}$ feet, what is the diameter? _____

3. If $3x + 4x - 4x = 36$, then $x =$ _____.

4. Write $\frac{1}{10^2}$ using exponents. _____

5. Simplify: $\dfrac{a^2 \cdot a \cdot b}{a \cdot a \cdot b} =$

6. $\begin{bmatrix} 2 & 3 \\ 1 & 5 \end{bmatrix} + \begin{bmatrix} 1 & 2 \\ 3 & 4 \end{bmatrix} =$

7. A room measures 12 feet by 10 feet. Thirty yards of trim have been ordered to go around the room.
    Has enough trim been ordered?   Circle: Yes   or   No

8. If $y = x^2 + x - 1$, find y if $x = 3$. $y =$ _____

9. $3\left|\dfrac{-1}{2}\right| =$ =

10. Write 0.00028 in scientific notation. _____

Eighth-Grade Math Minutes © 2007 Creative Teaching Press

MINUTE 48

1. How would you find the area of a pizza?

   a. $\varpi(r)^2$ **b.** $\varpi(d)$ **c.** $(\varpi)^2 r$ **d.** $(\varpi)^2 d$

2. How would you find the perimeter of a pizza?

   a. $\varpi(r)^2$ **b.** $\varpi(d)$ **c.** $(\varpi)^2 r$ **d.** $(\varpi)^2 d$

3. If the diameter of a circle is 11 cm, what is the radius? _____

4. Write $\dfrac{1}{8^3}$ using exponents. _____

5. If $x = -2$, what does y equal if $y = x^3 + 7$? _____

6. $\begin{bmatrix} -1 & 2 \\ -2 & 3 \end{bmatrix} - \begin{bmatrix} 1 & 2 \\ 3 & -3 \end{bmatrix} =$

7. Reduce: $\dfrac{a^3 \bullet a}{a^2} =$

Use >, <, or = to complete Problems 8–10.

8. x^2 _____ x^3 (If x is 2)

9. x^2 _____ x^3 (If x is –2)

10. $\dfrac{4}{5}$ _____ $\left(\dfrac{1}{4}\right)^2$

MINUTE 49

1. Round $0.\overline{7}$ to the nearest tenth. _____

Use the triangle to complete Problems 2–3.

2. What is the area? _____

3. What is the perimeter? _____

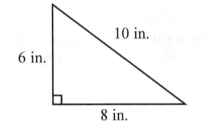

10 in.

6 in.

8 in.

4. $\dfrac{1}{10^2} \cdot \dfrac{10^2}{1} =$

5. $\begin{bmatrix} 4 \\ 8 \\ -3 \end{bmatrix} + \begin{bmatrix} -2 \\ -5 \\ -3 \end{bmatrix} =$

6. $\dfrac{4}{5}$ of 35 =

7. If $x^3 = 125$, what does x equal? _____

Use >, <, or = to complete Problems 8–10.

8. $\dfrac{4}{5}$ _____ 2^{-3}

9. 0.6 _____ 0.5

10. Mode of {1, 2, 2, 3, 3, 3, 14} _____ Mean of {1, 2, 2, 3, 3, 3, 14}

Eighth-Grade Math Minutes © 2007 Creative Teaching Press

MINUTE 50

1. Round $14.\overline{6}$ to the nearest tenth. _____

2. Simplify: $\frac{1}{3} + =$ _____

Use the figure to complete Problems 3–4.

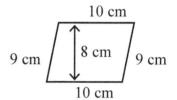

3. Find the area of the parallelogram. _____

4. Find the perimeter of the parallelogram. _____

Match each word with its definition to complete Problems 5–10.

5. Integer   **a.** average of a set of numbers

6. Rational number   **b.** number that occurs more than any other number in a set of numbers

7. Irrational number   **c.** positive or negative whole number, or zero

8. Mean   **d.** number in the middle of a set of numbers that are in numerical order

9. Median   **e.** number that can be written as a fraction like $\frac{a}{b}$

10. Mode   **f.** number that cannot be written as a fraction

1. If $t = 3$, then $3t^2 - t =$ _____ .

2. Reduce: $\dfrac{6 \cdot a \cdot a \cdot b}{a \cdot b} =$

3. The perimeter and circumference of a circle are the same.

Circle: True   or   False

4. $\sqrt{4 \cdot 16} =$

5. Find the volume of the box. _____

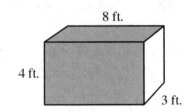

8 ft.

4 ft.

3 ft.

6. Which of these could be the volume of a shape?

    a. 16 m   **b.** 22 m^2 **c.** 36 m^3 **d.** 11 m^4

7. What is the area of a square with a side length of 12 cm? _____

8. $8^2 \cdot 8^{-2} =$

9. $\dfrac{4}{5}$ of 24 =

10. In general, as people get older, their income increases until they retire. Which of the graphs illustrates this statement? _____

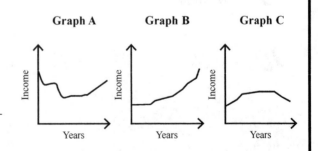

Graph A   Graph B   Graph C

Eighth-Grade Math Minutes © 2007 Creative Teaching Press

NAME: _____

MINUTE 52

1. If a triangle has a base of 6 feet and a height of 5 feet, what is the area? _____

2. If $5(x + 2) = 5x + 10$, then $6(x + 3) =$ _____.

3. Which measurement is the greatest?

    a. 1 yd.^3 **b.** 1 ft.^3 **c.** 1 m^3 **d.** 1 in.^3

4. If the volume of the box is 30 ft.^3, what is x? _____

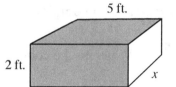

5. Round $0.\overline{42}$ to the nearest hundredth. _____

6. What is x if $3^x = 27$? _____

7. What is x if $3^x = \dfrac{1}{10}$? _____

Use >, <, or = to complete Problems 8–10.

8. 2^{-2} _____ $\dfrac{4}{5}$

9. 14.7 _____ $14.\overline{6}$

10. a positive times a negative _____ a negative times a negative

BONUS! If last month was July, what month will it be 21 months from now? _____

MINUTE 53

1. What is the missing angle of the triangle? _____

2. List the factors of 18. _____

3. $\left(\dfrac{-1}{6}\right)\left(\dfrac{4}{8}\right) =$

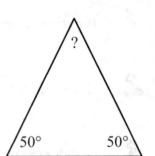

Use the graph to complete Problems 4–7.

4. What are the coordinates for point P? _____

5. What are the coordinates for point T? _____

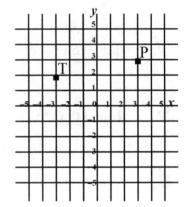

6. In what quadrant is point T located? _____

7. If you draw a line from point T to point P,
would the line have a positive or negative slope? _____

Complete the table for Problems 8–10.

n	$3n - 5$
3	
2	
1	

8.

9.

10.

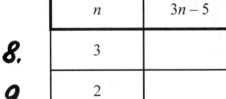

BONUS! How many rectangles are in this shape? _____

Eighth-Grade Math Minutes © 2007 Creative Teaching Press

MINUTE 54

1. What is the missing angle of the triangle? _____

2. What is the greatest common factor of 12 and 18? _____

3. What are the first three multiples of 7? _____

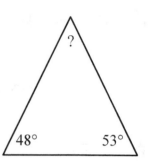

Use the graph to complete Problems 4–7.

4. What are the coordinates of points P and G? _____

5. What is the distance between points P and G? _____

6. In which quadrant is point G located? _____

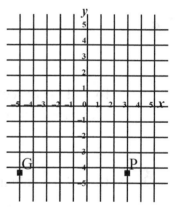

7. If point P is slid (translated) 4 units to the right, what would the new coordinates be? _____

Use $f(n) = n^2 - 2$ to complete Problems 8–10.

	n	f(n)
8.	2	
9.	1	
10.	−2	

MINUTE 55

1. How many degrees are in a triangle? _____

2. What is the greatest common factor of 10 and 30? _____

3. $\sqrt{49} =$

4. $\sqrt{36} =$

5. To find the area of a circle, multiply 3.14 by the radius.

    Circle: True   or   False

6. To find the volume of a box, multiply the length by the width by the height.

    Circle: True   or   False

7. $\sqrt{\dfrac{4}{25}} =$

Use $f(n) = 10 - n^2$ to complete Problems 8–10.

n	$f(n)$
8. 1	
9. 3	
10. 5	

Eighth-Grade Math Minutes © 2007 Creative Teaching Press

MINUTE 56

1. $\left[2 \cdot 2(2+1)\right]^2 =$

2. $-\sqrt{64} =$

3. $5 \pm \sqrt{49} =$

4. $3\begin{bmatrix} 3 \\ -8 \\ 6 \end{bmatrix} =$

5. To find the volume of a cylinder, multiply 3.14 by the radius times the height.

   Circle: True   or   False

6. To find the area of a triangle, multiply the length by the width.

   Circle: True   or   False

7. $\sqrt{\dfrac{64}{81}} =$

Use $f(n) = \sqrt{n^2} + n$ to complete Problems 8–10.

	n	f(n)
8.	1	
9.	4	
10.	16	

MINUTE 57

1. Is $\sqrt{60}$ closer to 7 or 8? _____

2. $\pm\sqrt{81} =$

3. $-2 \pm \sqrt{49} =$

4. The circumference of a circle is approximately 3.14 times the diameter?
　　Circle:　True　or　False

5. $-\sqrt{\dfrac{121}{144}} =$

6. Are these ratios proportionate: $\dfrac{6}{15}$ *and* $\dfrac{18}{45}$? Circle:　Yes　or　No

7. If $n^2 = 100$, what does n equal? _____

Use $f(n) = n^3 + n$ **to complete Problems 8–10.**

n	f(n)
1	
5	
-2	

8.

9.

10.

MINUTE 58

1. Is $\sqrt{60}$ closer to 7 or 8? _____

2. If $3^2 + 4^2 = c^2$, then $c =$ _____.

3. $-10 \pm \sqrt{121} =$

4. $-3 + (-4) \cdot 5 + 10 =$

5. Write 0.038383838 using bar notation. _____

6. $2\begin{bmatrix} 2 & 3 \\ 1 & 5 \end{bmatrix} + \begin{bmatrix} 1 & 2 \\ 3 & 4 \end{bmatrix} =$

7. $3^2 - 4(-2 + 5) =$

Use $d = 16t^2$ to complete Problems 8–10.

	d	t
8.		1
9.	64	
10.		−1

BONUS!

Which of the following is closest in value to 1?

a. $\dfrac{100}{99}$ **b.** $\dfrac{100}{99}$ **c.** $\left(\dfrac{99}{100}\right)^2$ **d.** $1 - 0.1^3$

Eighth-Grade Math Minutes © 2007 Creative Teaching Press

MINUTE 59

1. The symbol $\sqrt{}$ is called a(n) _____.

    a. division sign   **b.** exponent sign   **c.** radical sign   **d.** hypotenuse

2. When you add the length of any two sides of a triangle,
the result must be greater than the length of the third side.
Based on this statement, can these measurements be correct: 4 ft. x 5 ft. x 11ft.?

    Circle: Yes   or   No

3. Find the area of a 12 by 4 rectangle. _____

4. Round 6.2845 to the nearest hundredth. _____

5. What are the first five digits of the number $2.\overline{07}$? _____

6. Round the answer to Problem 5 to the nearest tenth. _____

7. Which measurement is greater?

    Circle: degrees in a triangle   or   an acute angle

8. $3 \cdot \left(\pm \sqrt{9} \right) =$

9. If $6^2 + b^2 = 10^2$, then $b =$ _____.

10. On a coordinate plane, what quadrant is the point (–3, –5) located? _____

Eighth-Grade Math Minutes © 2007 Creative Teaching Press

MINUTE 60

1. A(n) _____ number can always be written as a fraction or as a repeating decimal.

    a. irrational   **b.** rational   **c.** integer   **d.** whole

2. Can 5 cm, 5 cm, and 8 cm be the correct side length measurements of a triangle?   Circle: Yes   or   No

3. What type of triangle is described in Problem 2? _____

4. In a right triangle, Pythagoras discovered that $a^2 + b^2 = c^2$.
Which of the following measurements could be the sides of a right triangle?

    a. 1, 4, 5   **b.** 2, 3, 5   **c.** 4, 5, 6   **d.** 5, 12, 13

5. $\dfrac{4}{7} \div \dfrac{3}{7} =$

6. Put these numbers in order from least to greatest: 0.43, 4.3, 4.03, 0.043

    a. 0.43, 0.043, 4.3, 4.03   **b.** 0.043, 0.43, 4.3, 4.03

    c. 0.043, 0.43, 4.03, 4.3   **d.** 4.3, 4.03, 0.43, 0.043

7. The _____ is the longest side of a right triangle.

    a. hypotenuse   **b.** leg   **c.** Pythagorean theorem

8. What is the GCF of 24 and 8? _____

9. What is the LCM of 24 and 8? _____

10. If $\dfrac{1}{2}x - 4 = -2$ then $x =$ _____.

MINUTE 61

1. Which of these shapes is not a polygon?

    a. ▭   **b.** ◼   **c.** ●   **d.** ⬡

2. A paper clip might be measured best using:

    a. meters   **b.** kilometers   **c.** miles   **d.** centimeters

3. To measure a highway, use:

    a. meters   **b.** liters   **c.** grams

Use the prism to complete Problems 4–5.

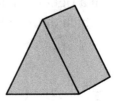

4. How many <u>faces</u> does the prism have?

    a. 5   **b.** 6   **c.** 8   **d.** 12

5. How many <u>edges</u> does the prism have?

    a. 5   **b.** 6   **c.** 7   **d.** 9

6. If $\dfrac{m}{5} > 4$, then $m >$ _____.

7. Does the ordered pair $(-2, -3)$ solve the equation $y = -5x - 7$?

    Circle: Yes   or   No

8. $\dfrac{1}{3} + \dfrac{1}{5} =$

Use the set of rays to complete Problems 9–10.

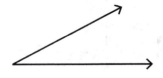

9. These rays form what type of angle?

    a. acute   **b.** obtuse   **c.** right

10. The two rays are _____.

    a. parallel   **b.** perpendicular   **c.** intersecting

Eighth-Grade Math Minutes © 2007 Creative Teaching Press

MINUTE 62

Use the prism to complete Problems 1–2.

1. How many <u>faces</u> does the prism have?

    a. 8   **b.** 6   **c.** 12   **d.** 10

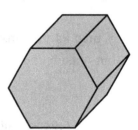

2. How many <u>edges</u> does the prism have?

    a. 10   **b.** 16   **c.** 12   **d.** 18

3. To measure volume, you use meters.

    Circle: True   or   False

4. Perpendicular lines form right angles.   Circle: True   or   False

5. Are $x = 4$ and $y = 8$ solutions of the equation: $y = x^2 - 2x + 1$?

    Circle: Yes   or   No

6. What type of lines are these?

    Circle: parallel   or   perpendicular

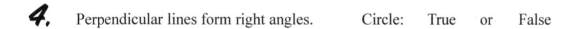

7. Which fraction is equal to 0.125?

    a. $\dfrac{4}{5}$ **b.** $\dfrac{4}{5}$ **c.** $\dfrac{1}{2}$ **d.** $\dfrac{4}{5}$

8. $0°$ Celsius = _____ $°$ Fahrenheit

9. 1 gallon = _____ quarts

10. These lines form what type of an angle?

    a. acute   **b.** obtuse   **c.** right

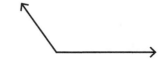

Eighth-Grade Math Minutes © 2007 Creative Teaching Press

MINUTE 63

Use the diagram to complete Problems 1–4.

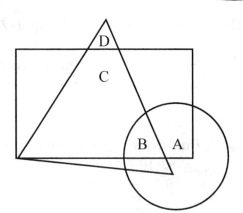

1. Which letter is inside the circle but outside the triangle? _____

2. Which letter is outside the rectangle but inside the triangle? _____

3. Which letter is in all three shapes? _____

4. Which letter is outside the circle but inside the triangle and rectangle? _____

5. How many vertices does this shape have? _____

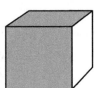

6. Solve $y = -2x + 4$ if $x = 3$. $y =$ _____

7. 1 yard = _____ inches

8. If $\frac{g}{2} + 2 = 5$, then $g =$ _____.

9. These lines form what type of an angle?
    a. right   **b.** obtuse   **c.** acute

10. What type of shape is this?
    a. pyramid   **b.** prism

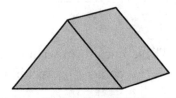

Eighth-Grade Math Minutes © 2007 Creative Teaching Press

MINUTE 64

Use the diagram to complete Problems 1–2.

1. Which letter is inside all three shapes?

2. Which letter is inside a circle, but outside the triangle?

3. Lines that cross are:
    a. intersecting   **b.** parallel   **c.** obtuse

4. Lines that are the same distance away from each other at all times are:
    a. intersecting   **b.** parallel   **c.** perpendicular

5. What type of triangle is this?
    a. isosceles   **b.** equilateral   **c.** scalene

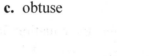

6. A triangle that has 3 noncongruent sides is a(n) _____ triangle.
    a. isosceles   **b.** equilateral   **c.** scalene

7. If $f(x) = (x + 3)^2$, find $f(2)$. _____

8. What comes next in the pattern: a, b, b, a, a, b, _____?

9. Which equation describes the data in the table?
    a. $y = -2x + 1$ **b.** $y = x + 1$
    c. $y = -x + 3$ **d.** $y = x - 5$

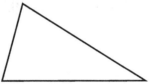

x	y
–2	5
1	2
4	–1
6	–3

10. How many sides does a decagon have?
    a. 5   **b.** 8   **c.** 10   **d.** 12

MINUTE 65

1. What type of lines are these?
  Circle: Parallel   or   Perpendicular

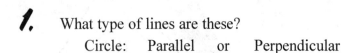

2. What type of lines are these?
  Circle: Parallel   or   Perpendicular   or   Intersecting

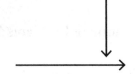

3. Does $x = 16$ solve the equation $5(x - 2) - 3(x + 4) = 10$?
  Circle: Yes   or   No

4. The perimeter of this shape is _____ in.

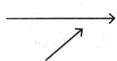

10 in.

5 in.   5 in.

10 in.

5. $5(2x + 13) =$

6. If $x + y = 12$ and $x - y = 4$, find x and y for both equations
  if the values given x and y are the same in both equations. _____

7. What kind of an angle is formed when a clock reads 2:00? _____

8. A triangle with all sides equal is called scalene.
  Circle: True   or   False

9. The perimeter of a room could be:
  a. 40 feet   **b.** 40 inches   **c.** 40 kilometers

10. What is the sum of the number of faces and edges in a cube? _____

Eighth-Grade Math Minutes © 2007 Creative Teaching Press

MINUTE 66

1. Draw an equilateral triangle.

2. Is $x = 3$ a solution for the equation $\dfrac{x-2}{x+1} = \dfrac{1}{4}$?   Circle: Yes   or   No

3. To find the distance around a yard, you need to know the _____.
     Circle: perimeter   or   area

Use the set of lines to complete Problems 4–5.

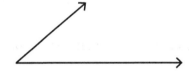

4. Which angle measurement could represent this angle?
     a. 45°   **b.** 90°   **c.** 130°

5. What type of angle do the two rays form?
     a. obtuse   **b.** right   **c.** acute

6. Solve for x. If $x^2 - 2 = 34$, then $x =$ _____.

7. $3(-4x - 5) =$

Use the shape to complete Problems 8–9.

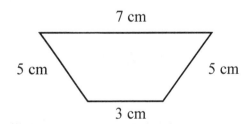

8. What is the name of the shape? _____

9. What is the perimeter of the shape? _____

10. Solve for x. If $2x + 5x - 4x = 33$, then $x =$ _____.

MINUTE 67

1. If $\dfrac{2x}{3} = \dfrac{8}{4}$, then $x =$ _____.

2. Which of the following could be the area of a shape?
   a. 18 ft.   **b.** 12 m   **c.** 25 in.^{2} **d.** 7 mm^3

3. Which of the following could be the perimeter of a shape?
   a. 25 in.^{2} **b.** 12 m   **c.** 18 ft.^{2} **d.** 7 mm^3

For each angle, write _acute_, _obtuse_, or _right_ to complete Problems 4–6.

4. ∠ COD _____

5. ∠ AOD _____

6. ∠ AOE _____

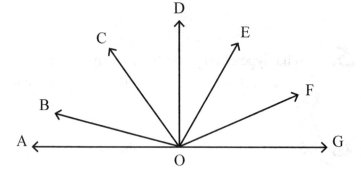

7. Draw the line(s) of symmetry.

8. Find $f(-2)$ if $f(x) = x^2 + x + 7$. $f(-2) =$

9. What is the diameter of a circle with the radius of 6.5 inches? _____

10. $-4(2x - 6) =$

Eighth-Grade Math Minutes © 2007 Creative Teaching Press

MINUTE 68

Use the diagram to complete Problems 1–4.

1. Which letters represent the diameter?
   - **a.** AO
   - **b.** DE
   - **c.** OB
   - **d.** AC

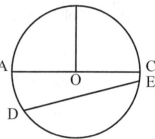

2. Which letters represent the radius?
   - **a.** DE
   - **b.** AD
   - **c.** AO
   - **d.** BC

3. Which letters represent a chord?
   - **a.** OB
   - **b.** DE
   - **c.** AO
   - **d.** OC

4. OB and OC are equal in length.   Circle: True   or   False

5. Find the area of the square on the right. _____

6. Find the perimeter of the square on the right. _____

   3.5 ft.

7. Use +, −, and • to complete the equation:

   4 _____ 5 _____ 2 _____ 6 = 8

8. Draw the line(s) of symmetry.

9. If all the sides of a triangle are equal, it is a(n) _____ triangle.
   - **a.** isosceles
   - **b.** scalene
   - **c.** equilateral

10. What type of triangle is this?

    _____

  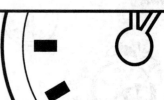

MINUTE 69

1. What is the area of the triangle? _____   4 in.

7 in.

2. Solve for x. If $4x + 12 + 8 - 10 = 30$, then $x =$ _____.

3. Which of these formulas is used to find the area of a triangle?

   a. $A = bh$ **b.** $A = lwh$ **c.** $A = \frac{1}{2}bh$ **d.** $A = l + w$

4. $3^2 + 4^2 = 5^2$ Circle: True or False

5. Which of the following formulas is used to find the circumference of a circle?

   a. $C = p + r$ **b.** $C = pd$ **c.** $C = dr$ **d.** $C = p$

6. $p \approx$

7. $\sqrt{49} =$

Match each description with the correct word to the right to complete Problems 8-10.

8. _____ All sides of a triangle are equal   **a.**   isosceles

9. _____ All sides of a triangle are different   **b.**   equilateral

10. _____ Two sides of a triangle are the same   **c.**   scalene

BONUS! Find a number that solves $x^2 - 6x + 9 = 0$. _____

Eighth-Grade Math Minutes © 2007 Creative Teaching Press

MINUTE 70

Use the number line to complete Problems 1–4.

1. Which letter is located at –2? _____

2. Which letter is located at 5? _____

3. Which number represents the letter E? _____

4. Which letter is halfway between F and L? _____

5. Write a mathematical statement to represent:
five times a number is less than 14. _____

6. $-6 > 2$ Circle: True or False

Use $x = 6$, $y = 4$, and $z = 3$ to complete Problems 7–10.

7. $4(x + y) =$

8. $4 + x \div 3 =$

9. $\frac{1}{2}yz =$

10. $y^2 =$

MINUTE 71

1. $3 \times 8 \neq 8 + 3 + 5$ Circle: True   or   False

2. The number 7 is all of the following except a(n):

    a. whole number   **b.** integer   **c.** natural number   **d.** irrational number

3. Which letters represent fractions on the number line? _____

4. If $a = 6$, then $2a^2 + 3 =$ _____.

5. $a \times 0 = a$ Circle: True   or   False

6. Circle the number that is the greatest: –5   –8   –2   –20

7. $11(2b - 3) =$

8. $8 + 4 = 3(4)$ Circle: True   or   False

9. $(2g)^2 =$

10. What should x be for this problem to be true: $2 + 3 + x = 1 + 8 - 2$? $x =$ _____

BONUS!

If the length, width, and height of a box are doubled, by how much does the volume increase? _____

Eighth-Grade Math Minutes © 2007 Creative Teaching Press

MINUTE 72

1. $-(8 + 3) =$

2. $(1 + 3) \times 5 = 1 + (3 \times 5)$ Circle: True   or   False

3. Simplify: $12b - 5b + 6b - 20b =$

4. If n is a positive number, then $-n$ is a _____ number.

5. $5y \cdot 71y \cdot 2y =$

6. If m is a positive number, arrange the fractions
   in order from least to greatest: $\dfrac{m}{4}, \dfrac{m}{8}, \dfrac{m}{3}$. _____

Use >, <, or = to complete Problems 7–10.

7. $-(-5)$ _____ -4

8. $-4(4)$ _____ -15

9. $4(2b + 7)$ _____ $8b + 28$

10. $|-8|$ _____ 6

MINUTE 73

1. Arrange the numbers in ascending order: 3.75, $3\frac{1}{4}$, $3\frac{1}{4}$. _____

2. $18 - 2(x + 3) =$

3. $4(7 - 5)^2 =$

4. $-(-2d) =$

5. $\left|\frac{1}{2}\right| + \left|\frac{-1}{2}\right| =$

6. $2g(3g)(4g) =$

7. $[3 - (-4)] + 2 =$

8. If $y = 4$, what is $y + (-3) + 6$? _____

Use the graph to complete Problems 9–10.

9. Where does the graph cross the y-axis? _____

10. Where does the graph cross the x-axis? _____

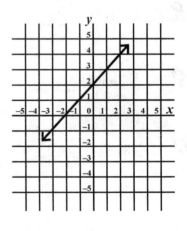

Eighth-Grade Math Minutes © 2007 Creative Teaching Press

MINUTE 74

1. $|(-5) + 3| =$

2. Simplify the expression: $2(2x + 3x) =$

3. Use the diagram to determine the correct equation solving for x.

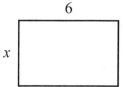

Area = 24

    a. $x + 6 = 24$ **b.** $6x = 24$

    c. $x + x + 6 + 6 = 24$ **d.** $2(x + 6) = 24$

4. If $|m| = 4$, then what two numbers can m equal? _____

5. $5 + |-6| > 9$ Circle: True   or   False.

6. Simplify the expression: $4y - 3y + 2 + 3 =$

Match each phrase with the correct expression to complete Problems 7–10.

7. A loss of 6 yards   **a.** n^2

8. The difference of a number and 3   **b.** -6

9. A number squared   **c.** $2n + 3y$

10. Two times a number plus 3 times a different number   **d.** $n - 3$

BONUS!

Barney averages 88% through four tests.
What does he need on the fifth test to raise his average to 90%? _____

Eighth-Grade Math Minutes © 2007 Creative Teaching Press

NAME: _____

MINUTE 75

1. Which member of $B = \{5, 9, 13, 25\}$ is divisible by 3? _____

2. What is the mean of set B in Problem 1? _____

3. Simplify: $5 + 3m + 4 + 9m =$

Use the graph to complete Problems 4–5.

4. What is the y-intercept? _____

5. What is the x-intercept? _____

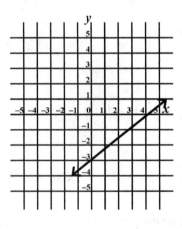

6. Fifteen less than –3 is _____.

7. If $2d + 10 = 50$, what does d equal? _____

Use $a = 2$, $b = 3$, and $c = 4$ to complete Problems 8–10.

8. $(3a)(b) =$

9. $2(5a) =$

10. $2c + 3c =$

BONUS!
How many different outfits can be made from 3 shirts, 4 pants, 2 belts, and 2 hats? _____

Eighth-Grade Math Minutes © 2007 Creative Teaching Press

NAME:

MINUTE 76

Use the graph to complete Problems 1–3.

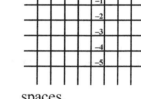

1. Draw point P at (–3, 2).

2. Draw point T at (2, 4).

3. To get from point P to point T, you must go up _____ spaces and right _____ spaces.

4. If $n = 3(4 - 7)^2$, then $n =$ _____ .

5. Find $A \cap B$, if $A = \{2,4,6,8,10\}$ and $B = \{3,6,9,12\}$. _____
(Hint: Which number is in set A and B?)

Simplify by combining like terms to complete Problems 6–10.

6. $10 + 5 + a + 4a =$

7. $10b - b =$

8. $-2c + 5c + 25c =$

9. $10b + 5(b + 2) =$

10. $12x + 2x - 17x =$

Eighth-Grade Math Minutes © 2007 Creative Teaching Press

MINUTE 77

1. $\dfrac{2}{9} + \dfrac{3}{9} =$

2. $\dfrac{1}{b} + \dfrac{2}{b} =$

3. If A = {1, 2, 3, 4, 5} and B = {5, 10, 15, 20}, find A ∩ B. _____

4. If $n^2 = 49$, what is n? _____

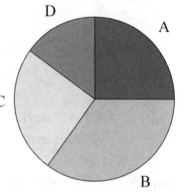

5. Based on the graph, category A represents _____.
   a. 10%   **b.** 50%   **c.** 70%   **d.** 25%

6. If $\dfrac{2}{8} = \dfrac{5}{x}$, then $x =$ _____.

7. Simplify: $4a + 2a - 6a =$

8. Which of these expression matches the phrase *a number squared plus 4*?
   a. $2n + 4$ **b.** $\sqrt{n} + 2$ **c.** $n + n + 4$ **d.** $n^2 + 4$

9. Which of the following numbers will solve $a^2 + 2 = 11$?
   a. 3   **b.** 4   **c.** 5   **d.** 0

10. Find n if $3n = 27 + 3$. $n =$ _____

Eighth-Grade Math Minutes © 2007 Creative Teaching Press

MINUTE 78

1. The reciprocal of $\dfrac{4t}{3}$ is _____.

2. $\dfrac{3}{d} + \dfrac{4}{d} =$

3. Which letter on the line graph represents $\dfrac{1}{2}$? _____

4. $\dfrac{5s}{8} - \dfrac{2s}{8} =$

5. Write an equation for the following phrase:
3 times a number plus 6 equals 9. _____

6. Which of the following does not solve the inequality $x > -4$?
    Circle: 2   5 -10 $|x|$

7. Which element of S $= \{1, 2, 3, 4, 5\}$ solves this equation: $3r + r = 16$? _____

8. Which phrase describes $2(n + 5)$?
    a. A number increased by 5   **b.** Two times the difference of a number and 5
    c. Two plus a number plus 5   **d.** Two times the sum of a number and 5

9. $(-3w)(-2w)(-4w) =$

10. If $n = 3$, then $n^2 = 3n$.   Circle: True   or   False

MINUTE 79

1. If A = {5, 6, 7, 8, 9} and B = {prime numbers}, what is A ∩ B? _____

2. $(2a)(-5a)(4a^2) =$

3. What is the solution of $|x| > 5$?
   a. All numbers greater than 5
   b. All numbers less than 5
   c. All numbers greater than 5 and all numbers less than −5

4. $\dfrac{1}{2} \div \dfrac{2a}{3} =$.

5. If Jill is n years old and Jack is 3 years older,
   which one of the following equations describes Jack's age?
   a. $n - 3$ b. $3n$ c. $n + 3$ d. n^2

6. What is the <u>coefficient</u> in $6y^4$? _____

7. What is the <u>exponent</u> in $6y^4$? _____

8. Evaluate $25 - 4y$, when $y = 5$. _____

9. Is n^2 always greater than n?   Circle: Yes   or   No

10. Is n^2 always greater than n for all whole numbers?   Circle: Yes   or   No

Eighth-Grade Math Minutes © 2007 Creative Teaching Press

MINUTE 80

1. $2a(3a + 4) = 6a^2 + 8a$ Circle: True   or   False

2. Simplify: $2a + 5a + 6a^2 =$

3. Is $(4, -14)$ a solution for the equation $y = -3x - 2$?   Circle: Yes   or   No

4. If $a = 2$, then $3 \cdot 4a = 12a$.   Circle: True   or   False

5. $\frac{1}{2}(4b + 8) =$

6. $5(4c) =$

7. If $a = b$ and $b = 2$, then $a =$ _____.

Write an equation for each phrase and solve it to complete Problems 8–10.

8. Four times a number is 40. _____

9. The sum of n and 4 is 20. _____

10. Half of a number is 10. _____

MINUTE 81

1. If AC is 11 inches and BC is 4 inches, then AB = _____.

A ————— B ——— C

2. $4b + 3b - 5b + 5 =$

3. $5(3g) =$

4. $3 \cdot 2 \cdot 5a =$

5. Write an equation for the following statement and then solve it: *three times a number plus 6 equals 12.* _____

6. $\dfrac{2}{3} \cdot \dfrac{2}{3} \cdot \dfrac{a}{1} =$

7. $5a + 6b + 4a - 2b =$

8. $\dfrac{-4}{2} =$

9. $\dfrac{-4}{-2} =$

10. What is the perimeter? _____

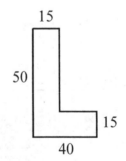

Eighth-Grade Math Minutes © 2007 Creative Teaching Press

MINUTE 82

1. The sum of a positive number and a negative number is always positive.
    Circle: True   or   False

Match each problem with the correct answer to complete Problems 2–6.

2. $5(y + b)$ **a.** $4y + 20$

3. $4y \cdot 5y$ **b.** $5y + 5b$

4. $10(5y) - 20y$ **c.** $18y^3$

5. $3y \cdot 2y \cdot 3y$ **d.** $30y$

6. $4(y + 5)$ **e.** $20y^2$

Use the graph to complete Problems 7–9.

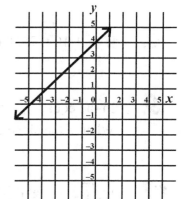

7. Is the point $(-5, 0)$ on the line?   Circle: Yes   or   No

8. Is the point $(0, 2)$ on the line?   Circle: Yes   or   No

9. Find the slope $\left(\frac{rise}{run}\right)$ of the line. _____

10. If a line on a graph goes up from left to right, the slope of the line is _____.
    Circle: positive   or   negative

Eighth-Grade Math Minutes © 2007 Creative Teaching Press

MINUTE 83

1. What is the coefficient in $7y^3$? _____

2. If $x = 2$ and $y = 3$, then $x^2y^2 =$ _____.

3. $3x + 6x = 18x^2$ Circle: True   or   False

4. $12x + 5x - 7x =$

5. For what integers is $n \times 4 > 10$? _____

6. Simplify: $5y + 6y - y =$

7. Evaluate $50 - 4y$ when $y = -3$. _____

8. If $5x + 10 = 25$, then solve for x. _____

9. In the equation $y = 3x + 7$, the slope is 3.
   What is the slope of the line $y = 4x - 2$? _____

10. If $\sqrt{y} - 2 = 8$, then $y =$ _____.

BONUS! What is the sum of the factors for the number 18? _____

Eighth-Grade Math Minutes © 2007 Creative Teaching Press

MINUTE 84

1. If $x = 5$, then $x^2 - x + 8 =$ _____.

2. If 5 more than n is 12, what is n? _____

3. Find the area of the triangle. _____

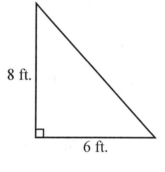

8 ft.

6 ft.

4. If $x + 6 = -2$, then $x =$ _____.

5. If $-3x = 27$, then $x =$ _____.

6. Simplify: $3y + 2y + 6y - 4x =$

7. What does $\frac{1}{2}x$ equal if x is 9? _____

Use the graph to complete Problems 8–10.

8. In how many places do the lines intersect? _____

9. In which quadrant do the lines intersect? _____

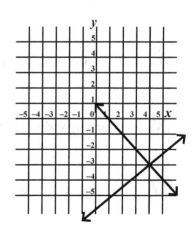

10. The lines intersect at _____.

Eighth-Grade Math Minutes © 2007 Creative Teaching Press

NAME:

MINUTE 85

1. If $5(x + 4) = 30$, then $x =$ _____.

2. If $6 = \frac{1}{3}x$, then $x =$ _____.

3. If $3x + 2x = 60$, then $x =$ _____.

4. If $x = 2$, then $\frac{10x}{x} = 10$.   Circle: True   or   False

5. Jason travels 20 miles east, turns around and travels 8 miles west. How far east did Jason actually end up from his starting position? _____

6. A positive times a negative equals a _____.

7. A negative times a negative equals a _____.

8. A positive divided by a negative equals a _____.

9. A negative divided by a negative equals a _____.

10. Complete the table on the right assuming that: $y = 4x + 2$.

x	y
2	
	6
	18

Eighth-Grade Math Minutes © 2007 Creative Teaching Press

MINUTE 86

1. $1^{48} =$

2. What is the maximum number of 33¢ stamps that can be purchased with $3? _____

3. What is the area of the rectangle that is beside the square? _____

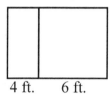

4 ft.   6 ft.

4. $4(2a + 8) =$

5. What is 20% of 40? _____

6. Jessica buys lollipops for $.25 and sells them for $.50. If she sells 10 lollipops, what is her profit? _____

7. $3(4x) - 2x =$

8. $9 + 3\frac{1}{2} + 2\frac{1}{2} =$

9. $\dfrac{16ab}{8} =$

10. $\dfrac{2a}{7} + \dfrac{3a}{7} =$

Eighth-Grade Math Minutes © 2007 Creative Teaching Press

MINUTE 87

1. $5(a + 3b) =$

2. $3x^2 + 2x^2 =$

3. $2 \cdot 3 \cdot 4 \cdot y \cdot y \cdot y =$

4. Find the number: *three times a number plus 8 is 38.* _____

5. If $6x + 9 + 3x = 45$, then $x =$ _____.

6. If $y^3 = 64$, what is y? _____

7. Find the lowest common denominator for the fractions $\frac{1}{3}$ and $\frac{3}{8}$. _____

8. Which of these will have the greatest value for all positive numbers "x"?

    a. $\dfrac{x}{0.5}$ **b.** $\dfrac{x}{0.05}$ **c.** $\dfrac{x}{0.005}$ **d.** $\dfrac{x}{0.0005}$

9. If $x = -2$ and $y = 4$, then $-x - xy =$ _____.

10. Which of the following is not the same as the others?

    a. 41%   **b.** 0.41   **c.** $-4\frac{2}{5}$ **d.** 0.041

Eighth-Grade Math Minutes © 2007 Creative Teaching Press

MINUTE 88

Name:

Use the diagram to complete Problems 1–2.

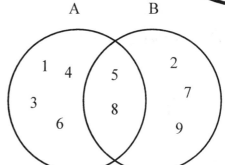

1. Find $A \cap B$. _____

2. What is the mean of $A \cap B$? _____

3. Write $9\frac{1}{2}\%$ as a decimal. _____

4. $\dfrac{10 \cdot 10 \cdot 10}{10 \cdot 10} =$

5. Which of these represents 3 times a number squared?

  a. $3n^2$ **b.** $3\sqrt{n}$ **c.** $3(2n)$ **d.** $3(n + n)$

6. $-[-(-4)] =$

7. Circle the number that is not prime: 11   13   17   22   29

8. $2(7 + 3)^3 =$

9. In the equation $|p| = 9$, what two numbers can p equal? _____

10. Complete the table on the right assuming that: $y = -2x + 8$.

x	y
	4
0	
−2	

Eighth-Grade Math Minutes © 2007 Creative Teaching Press

MINUTE 89

1. If $a = 5$, then $50 - 10 + 4a =$ _____ .

2. $\dfrac{2}{3} \cdot \dfrac{n}{y} \cdot \dfrac{5}{7} =$

3. $\dfrac{-3}{4} \times \dfrac{-a}{b} =$

4. If n represents an odd number, what equation would represent the next odd number?

    a. $2n$ **b.** $n + n$ **c.** $n + 2$ **d.** $n - 2$

5. If $2y + 3y = 35 - 5$, then $y =$ _____ .

6. Solve: $\dfrac{2b}{3} = 8$

7. $\dfrac{5ac}{d} + \dfrac{5ac}{d} =$

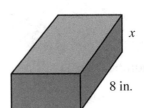

8. If the volume of this box is 80 in.^{3}, then what is the value of x? _____

Use the graph to complete Problems 9–10.

9. Which of these equations represents the graph?

    a. $y = x - 2$ **b.** $y = 2x + 2$

    c. $y = -5x + 2$ **d.** $y = -\dfrac{1}{2}x - 2$

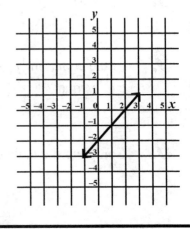

10. What is the y-intercept of the graph? _____

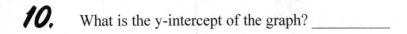

Eighth-Grade Math Minutes © 2007 Creative Teaching Press

MINUTE 90

1. If $a = 4$, then $a^2 =$ _____.

2. $4x(x + 3) =$

3. If $6x + 3x + 4 = 40$, then $x =$ _____.

4. What is m^2n^3 if $m = 5$ and $n = 2$? _____

5. Simplify: $5x^2y + 2x^2y - 4x^2y =$

6. Find angle B if angle A = 60°. _____

7. $x^2 \cdot x^4 \cdot x =$

8. $-3\sqrt{36} =$

9. $-(-4)^2 =$

10. What is $x(x - y) + xy$ if $x = -3$ and $y = -2$? _____

BONUS!

Which of these choices makes the best comparison,
STRAW is to WARTS as 6323 is to _____.

   a. 2336   **b.** 6232   **c.** 3236   **d.** 6332

Eighth-Grade Math Minutes © 2007 Creative Teaching Press

MINUTE 91

1. Solve for x: $3x + 2 = 8$. $x =$ _____

2. $12(x - 6) =$

3. $(-\sqrt{9})(3) =$

4. If $-x = 8$, then $x =$ _____.

5. Solve for x. $3x + 2x = 30$, $x =$ _____

6. $\dfrac{a \cdot a \cdot a}{a \cdot a \cdot b} =$

7. $12x \cdot x^2 \cdot 2x =$

8. Solve for x. $4x + 20 = 3x$, $x =$ _____

9. What is y if both triangles are proportional? _____

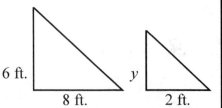

6 ft.   8 ft. y 2 ft.

10. $(4y)^2 =$

BONUS!

Leah likes the number 400 but not 500. She likes 900 but not 999. She likes 2,500 but not 600. Which of these numbers will she like?

a. 1,000   **b.** 1,100   **c.** 1,200   **d.** 1,600

Eighth-Grade Math Minutes © 2007 Creative Teaching Press

MINUTE 92

1. $\sqrt{16} - \sqrt{25} =$

2. Solve for x. $6x - 2x = 24$, $x =$ _____

3. $-5(x - 2) =$

4. If $-y = x + 6$, then $y =$ _____.

5. Solve for a. $-10a = 70$, $a =$ _____

6. $2x \cdot x \cdot 5x =$

7. $\dfrac{a}{c} + \dfrac{2}{c} =$

8. If $y = -3x + 6$, then the slope of this line is negative.
Circle: True   or   False

Use the graph to complete Problems 9–10.

9. Which of these equations describes the line in the graph?
a. $y = x + 3$ b. $y = x - 3$
c. $y = -x + 3$ d. $y = -x - 3$

10. Where does the line cross the x-axis? _____

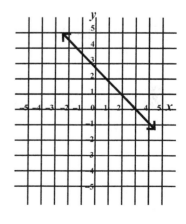

1. Is $x = 3$ a solution of the equation $3x + 1 = 5x - 5$?
   Circle: Yes   or   No

2. If $3x < 15$, then $x <$ _____.

3. $4x(x - 6) =$

4. If $-x = -7$, then $x =$ _____.

5. Does (2, 3) solve the equation $3x + 2y = 12$?   Circle: Yes   or   No

6. Solve for a: $-4a \le 12$. $a \ge$ _____

7. What is the slope of the line $y = 4x + 5$? _____

8. What is the y-intercept of the equation in problem 7? _____

x	y
2	5
4	9
7	15

9. Use the chart on the right to complete the function rule $y =$ ____ $x + 1$.

10. Using the function rule from Problem 9, find y if $x = 10$. _____

Eighth-Grade Math Minutes © 2007 Creative Teaching Press

MINUTE 94

1. If $|x| = 7$, then $x =$ _____ or $x =$ _____.

2. If $6x \geq 18$, then $x \geq$ _____.

3. Write an equation for the following statement and solve:
   six times a number plus 5 times the same number is 33. _____

4. Does $x = 15$ solve the equation $2x + 10 = 3x$?   Circle: Yes   or   No

5. Solve for x: $-7x - 1 < 6$. $x >$ _____

6. $5(a + b + c) =$

7. Solve for y: $y - 5 = x + 3$. $y =$ _____

8. Does $(-1, 1)$ solve the equation $2x + y = -3$?   Circle: Yes   or   No

9. If the volume of the cube is 27 in.^{3}, then what is x? _____

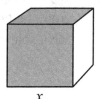

x

10. What is the surface area of the cube in Problem 9?

BONUS!
A boy is 5 years old and his sister is 3 times as old as he is.
When the boy is 18, how old will his sister be? _____

MINUTE 95

1. What is the slope of the equation $y = 3x - 8$? _____

2. What is the y-intercept of the equation above? _____

3. What is $f(3)$ if $f(x) = x^2 - x$? _____

4. Simplify: $3x(4x^2 - 8x + 2) =$

5. If $|x - 1| = 8$, then $x =$ _____ and _____.

6. Parallel lines have _____ slopes.
   a. the same   **b.** opposite   **c.** reciprocal

7. Complete the function rule for the table: $y = 4x +$ ____

x	y
1	5
-1	-3
0	1

Use the graph to complete problems 8–10.

8. If you graphed the x- and y-coordinates from the table in Problem 7 and connected the dots, what shape would you have? _____

9. In the first quadrant, the x and y values are both _____.
   Circle: positive   or   negative

10. In the third quadrant, the x and y values are both _____.
    Circle: positive   or   negative

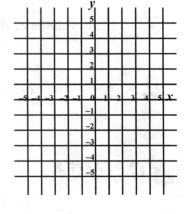

Eighth-Grade Math Minutes © 2007 Creative Teaching Press

MINUTE 96

1. Does $x = 3$ solve the equation $x^2 + 3x = 0$?   Circle: Yes   or   No

2. What is the slope of the equation: $y = -13x + 8$? _____

3. What is the y-intercept of the equation in Problem 2? _____

4. If $y = 3x$, what is the range given the domain of $\{2, 3, 5\}$? _____

5. $a^2(a)(a^3) =$

6. Solve: $3x > -9$. x > _____

Match the problem with the correct answer to complete for Problems 7–10,

7. $x - 3 = -7$ **a.** $x = 1$

8. $\sqrt{x} = 4$ **b.** $x = -4$

9. $\dfrac{x}{2} = 4$ **c.** $x = 16$

10. $2x - 6 = -4$ **d.** $x = 8$

BONUS!
If all ziggles are zoogles and all zoogles are zaggles, do all ziggles have to be zaggles?   Circle: Yes   or   No

MINUTE 97

Use the rectangle to complete Problems 1–3.

1. What is the area? _____

3

2. What is the perimeter? _____

$x + 5$

3. If the area of the rectangle is 21m^2, what is x? _____

4. $(4x^2 + 8)6 =$

5. $-\left[-(-5)\right] = -5$ Circle: True   or   False

6. $-a^2 = (-a)^2$ Circle: True   or   False

7. $\dfrac{b^4 c^3}{b^2} =$

8. Solve: $-2x < 9. \ x >$ _____

9. $\dfrac{r}{10} = \dfrac{21}{7}$ $r =$ _____

10. 60 is 75% of what number? _____

4	32	144
17	28	122
18	64	188
322	14	200

BONUS! Which number does not belong in the chart?

Eighth-Grade Math Minutes © 2007 Creative Teaching Press

MINUTE 98

1. What is the area of the rectangle? _____

4x

2. What is the perimeter of the rectangle? _____

x − 2

3. If $2x + 8 = 3x$, does $x = 8$ solve the equation?   Circle: Yes   or   No

Use the graph to complete Problems 4–7.

4. In which quadrant is the point $(x, 3)$ if $x < 0$? _____

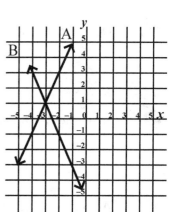

5. At what coordinates do the lines intersect? _____

6. Does line A have a positive or negative slope? _____

7. Which of these could be the equation for line B?

   a. $y = -2x - 5$ **b.** $y = -2x + 5$

   c. $y = 2x + 5$ **d.** $y = 2x + 5$

Circle the best estimate to complete Problems 8–10.

8. 18% of 50   **a.** 1   **b.** 10   **c.** 100

9. 75% of 250   **a.** 18   **b.** 180   **c.** 1,800

10. 200% of 800   **a.** 15   **b.** 150   **c.** 1,600

MINUTE 99

1. Given the line $y = 3(x + 2)$, what is the slope? _____

2. What is the y-intercept of the line in Problem 1? _____

3. Is the point (1, 9) on the line in Problem 1? _____

4. Does the line in Problem 1 pass through the origin (0, 0)?
   Circle: Yes   or   No

5. How many solutions does the equation $|x| = -2$ have?
   a. 1   **b.** 1   **c.** none

6. A coin was flipped three times. What are the chances that all 3 flips resulted in heads? _____

7. A circle was divided into 3 pieces. Two of the pieces make up 200 degrees of the circle. How many degrees is the third piece? _____

Choose the best estimate to complete Problems 8–10.

8. 21 out of 60   **a.** 50%   **b.** 75%   **c.** 33%

9. 9% of 45   **a.** 5   **b.** 15   **c.** 25

10. 64%   **a.** $\frac{3}{4}$ **b.** $\frac{2}{3}$ **c.** $\frac{1}{2}$

Eighth-Grade Math Minutes © 2007 Creative Teaching Press

MINUTE 100

1. If $f(x) = x^2 + 1$, then $f(2) = $ _____.

2. How many solutions does the problem $3 = |x - 3|$ have? _____

3. If two lines have the same slope, they are _____.
       a. parallel   **b.** perpendicular   **c.** intersecting

4. If $x^2 = 400$, then $x = $ _____.

5. $\sqrt{7} \cdot \sqrt{7} = $

6. Write an equation to show *three times a number is 11.* _____

7. $a^3 \cdot a^4 = $

8. $(a^3)^2 = $

9. $\dfrac{a^5}{a^3}$

10. The area of the base of the cylinder is 40 cm^2.
    The height is 10 cm. What is the volume? _____

BONUS! Find one solution of three numbers that add up to 41. *Circle the numbers.*
      2   3   21   17   11   8   12   13

Eighth-Grade Math Minutes © 2007 Creative Teaching Press

MINUTE ANSWER KEY

MINUTE 1
1. 8
2. 6
3. 35
4. 14
5. 36
6. 3^4
7. 72
8. 8
9. 1
10. 17

BONUS: 5 pigs, 2 chickens

MINUTE 2
1. 24
2. 4^5
3. 2
4. $5^2 = 25$
5. True
6. 30
7. a
8. 24
9. 59
10. c

MINUTE 3
1. 26
2. $4^4 \cdot 6^2$
3. 2
4. $4^2 = 4 \cdot 4, 2^4 = 2 \cdot 2 \cdot 2 \cdot 2$
5. 3,200
6. 18
7. 43
8. 42
9. 55
10. b

MINUTE 4
1. 3,570
2. $2^5 = 32$
3. a, d
4. a, b
5. c
6. 4
7. $\frac{1}{4}$
8. 3
9. 5
10. 51

MINUTE 5
1. False
2. 5.806×10^3
3. True
4. 8
5. 42
6. 3
7. x^3
8. 36
9. $2^2 = 4$
10. b

MINUTE 6
1. 14
2. 2.0136×10^4
3. $\frac{4}{9}$
4. True
5. 4
6. 20
7. Yes
8. 20
9. $4^2 = 16$
10. $\frac{1}{9}$

BONUS: 18

MINUTE 7
1. 5, −4, 100
2. 0.7
3. 3
4. 4
5. c
6. 24
7. $0.75
8. 70%
9. 4.2
10. 0

MINUTE 8
1. 3,064
2. $4^4 \cdot 8^2$
3. 56
4. 18
5. 2.6373×10^4
6. d
7. 46%
8. $1.20
9. 6.3
10. 64

MINUTE 9
1. 3
2. $\frac{1}{64}$
3. $7^2 = 49$
4. 406.8
5. 0.468
6. 32
7. Yes
8. 3.62×10^4
9. 48%
10. 7

BONUS: $2 + 3 + 5 + 7 + 11 = 28$

MINUTE 10
1. 23,000 pounds
2. 4.8
3. 5.9×10^3
4. $a^3 \cdot b^2 \cdot c$
5. 35%
6. 8^5
7. $\frac{1}{4}$
8. True
9. 10
10. c

MINUTE 11
1. −50, −25, −10, 10, 25
2. $9^2 = 81$
3. 150 $in.^2$
4. 6
5. −81
6. −5
7. 24%
8. >
9. <
10. >

BONUS: 4, 2, 3, 1 or 2, 4, 3, 1

MINUTE 12
1. 56
2. −1
3. 12, 8, 0, −3, −4
4. −80
5. 8.43×10^2
6. 216 $in.^3$
7. 36
8. True
9. 18
10. 24

BONUS: 8, 13, 21

MINUTE 13
1. True
2. 13
3. 24
4. 10
5. $\frac{1}{9}$
6. −22
7. −2
8. −15
9. −5
10. $\frac{1}{25}$

BONUS: 1, 5, 10, 10, 5, 1

MINUTE 14
1. 5
2. False
3. 1.407×10^3
4. 9
5. −10, 0, $|−11|$, 20
6. 2 hrs. 14 minutes
7. −2
8. 49
9. $4^6 = 4,096$
10. Negative (−)

MINUTE 15
1. 5
2. −20
3. −8
4. 20
5. −2
6. a
7. True
8. Positive (+)
9. True
10. 25

MINUTE 16
1. 18
2. −7
3. b
4. b
5. −16
6. −30
7. −32
8. −2
9. True
10. No

BONUS: 12

MINUTE 17
1. $\frac{2}{4}$
2. −5
3. 2
4. c
5. −17
6. d
7. 60
8. False
9. True
10. −3

MINUTE 18
1. 2
2. −6
3. 210
4. $7 loss
5. $\frac{11}{12}$
6. $−\frac{1}{12}$
7. True
8. −20
9. 14
10. a, c

BONUS: 25 hours

MINUTE 19
1. 0.38
2. −22
3. 25
4. 7
5. 4,380
6. $3^3 \cdot 4^3$
7. −2
8. No
9. −11
10. c

BONUS: $6,400

MINUTE 20
1. 0.2
2. −20
3. 11
4. 100
5. c
6. 0.36
7. a
8. 64
9. 30
10. 30

MINUTE ANSWER KEY

MINUTE 21
1. 13.28
2. 7
3. b
4. 0.1
5. $\frac{2}{15}$
6. Rational
7. 3.82×10^{-2}
8. 12
9. $8^2 = 64$
10. 12

MINUTE 22
1. $0.16, \frac{4}{25}$
2. 36
3. 75%
4. a
5. -8
6. 2.5
7. $0.12 \times 84 = n$
8. <
9. =
10. >

MINUTE 23
1. $3
2. 60
3. Yes
4. $\frac{3}{8}$
5. a, b
6. $(41 \div 55) \times 100 = s$
7. d
8. $\frac{1}{6}$
9. 15
10. $a^3 \cdot b^4$

MINUTE 24
1. 15
2. -6
3. 55 ft.
4. 7
5. a, b, d
6. b^4
7. b
8. $1.80
9. 60%
10. 32

MINUTE 25
1. 100
2. 15
3. Discount
4. False
5. b, c
6. $4
7. d
8. 20% of 400
9. 40
10. $\frac{11}{12}$
BONUS: Answers may vary.
Possible answer: 1Q, 2D, 4N

MINUTE 26
1. $\frac{9}{20}$
2. False
3. 25% of 500
4. $0.05, \frac{1}{10}, \frac{1}{5}, 25\%$
5. True
6. $-\frac{4}{9}$
7. $\frac{11}{3}$
8. $-\frac{1}{3}$
9. 70°
10. $4\frac{1}{2}$

MINUTE 27
1. $\frac{3}{10}$
2. True
3. $\frac{1}{20}, \frac{1}{8}, 15\%, 0.78$
4. True
5. 20
6. $-\frac{1}{5}$
7. $\frac{5}{6}$
8. $\frac{43}{4}$
9. 20% of 1,000
10. 2, 5, 7, 11

MINUTE 28
1. Second
2. a, b
3. 0.075
4. <
5. a, b
6. $\frac{1}{6}$
7. 4,007,400,000 cm
8. Irrational
9. $5 - (8 + 2) = -5$
10. $(5 \times 3) - (4 + 10) = 1$

MINUTE 29
1. True
2. 7
3. $-\frac{33}{4}$
4. 4.332×10^3
5. 32%
6. 0.025
7. 52%
8. d
9. $\frac{1}{8}$
10. Negative

MINUTE 30
1. False
2. -28
3. $\frac{3}{13}$
4. Rational
5. $-\frac{38}{3}$
6. $3
7. 3
8. 10
9. $\frac{1}{100}$
10. 78 sq. units
BONUS: 29

MINUTE 31
1. True
2. -18
3. $\frac{3}{16}$
4. 0.25, 25%
5. $-\frac{22}{5}$
6. $\frac{1}{5}$
7. $\frac{4}{25}$
8. 2
9. $-\frac{5}{8}$
10. $a = 12$

MINUTE 32
1. 15
2. $\frac{9}{56}$
3. $-\frac{5}{8}$
4. 2
5. 8.4×10^{-3}
6. 90
7. $\frac{1}{400}$
8. 60
9. -6
10. a

MINUTE 33
1. -42
2. 3
3. 9
4. $\frac{1}{64}$
5. 6
6. mean
7. 12
8. 3
9. $-13\frac{3}{5}$
10. 72

MINUTE 34
1. $\frac{9}{25}, 0.36$
2. a
3. -27
4. 4
5. 16
6. $\frac{3}{20}$
7. 51
8. $12^{-2} = \frac{1}{144}$
9. $x = 25$
10. $y = 11$

MINUTE 35
1. $11, 0, -5, -5\frac{1}{2}, -21$
2. 4.2×10^{-6}
3. -4
4. -9
5. 30%
6. $\frac{3}{10}$
7. 0.30 or 0.3
8. $\frac{50}{15}$
9. 7^{12}
10. a
BONUS: 400

MINUTE 36
1. $0, -7, -12, -15$
2. 3.4322×10^4
3. -16
4. 50
5. $-\frac{25}{11}$
6. $\frac{25}{11}$
7. 4^8
8. b
9. $\frac{3}{10}, 30\%$
10. 29

MINUTE 37
1. 6
2. 3,111
3. -36
4. $\frac{3}{13}$
5. Brittany
6. Jill
7. 20
8. $-\frac{36}{11}$
9. 5^{18}
10. $-\frac{7}{11}$
BONUS: 4

MINUTE 38
1. $\frac{3}{12}$ should be $\frac{4}{12}$
2. 20%
3. 50%
4. Nicole, Alicia
5. False
6. $\frac{1}{56}$
7. 14
8. Tuesday
9. About 22
10. c

MINUTE 39
1. $\frac{4}{21}$ should be $\frac{7}{21}$
2. 5
3. 4
4. 4
5. Spencer, Trent
6. No
7. Allisen
8. Andrew
9. -15
10. 36

MINUTE 40
1. March
2. Food
3. About $18
4. 3
5. 3
6. 3
7. 4
8. -19
9. $\frac{1}{49}$
10. $\frac{1}{a^2}$
BONUS: 4

MINUTE ANSWER KEY

MINUTE 41
1. 4 feet
2. a
3. About 5'1" tall
4. 10 years old
5. $m = 294$
6. $x = 7$
7. $d = 80$
8. $x = 64$
9. 63 feet
10. 30 *in.*

MINUTE 42
1. B
2. A
3. C
4. D
5. Yes
6. No
7. Mean
8. -4
9. $-\frac{19}{8}$
10. 6

MINUTE 43
1. 5
2. 24 cm
3. a
4. d
5. $\frac{1}{6}$
6. $\frac{1}{2}$
7. 22
8. $-\frac{6}{7}$
9. $\frac{1}{11}$
10. $\frac{2}{11}$

MINUTE 44
1. 40
2. 23 cm
3. c
4. a
5. 1, 2, 3, 5
6. $\frac{2}{3}$
7. 10.4
8. $\frac{9}{49}$
9. $\frac{1}{8}$
10. $\frac{1}{4}$

MINUTE 45
1. c
2. 56 in.
3. c
4. a
5. 5, 7, 11, 13
6. 16.5 ft.
7. 21, 28, 36
8. 1
9. $\frac{1}{3}$
10. $\frac{4}{9}$

MINUTE 46
1. 54 in. or $4\frac{1}{2}$ ft.
2. a
3. $8\frac{1}{2}$ feet
4. 1.5 cups
5. 5^{-2}
6. ab
7. False
8. No
9. $y = 50$
10. 20

MINUTE 47
1. 40 in.
2. $8\frac{1}{2}$ feet
3. $x = 12$
4. 10^{-2}
5. a
6. $\begin{bmatrix} 3 & 5 \\ 4 & 2 \end{bmatrix}$
7. Yes
8. $y = 11$
9. $\begin{bmatrix} 12 & 3 \\ 3 & 0 \end{bmatrix}$
10. 2.8×10^{-4}

MINUTE 48
1. a
2. b
3. $5\frac{1}{2}$ cm
4. 8^{-3}
5. $y = -1$
6. $\begin{bmatrix} -2 & 0 \\ -5 & 6 \end{bmatrix}$
7. a^2
8. $<$
9. $>$
10. $>$

MINUTE 49
1. 0.8
2. 24 *in.*²
3. 24 *in.*
4. 1
5. $\begin{bmatrix} 2 \\ 3 \\ -6 \end{bmatrix}$
6. 5
7. 5
8. $=$
9. $>$
10. $<$

MINUTE 50
1. 12.6
2. 11^3
3. 80 cm²
4. 38 cm
5. c
6. e
7. f
8. a
9. d
10. b

MINUTE 51
1. 24
2. $6a$
3. True
4. 8
5. 96 ft.³
6. c
7. 144 cm²
8. 1
9. 8
10. Graph B

MINUTE 52
1. 15 ft.²
2. $6x + 18$
3. c
4. 3 ft.
5. 0.42
6. 3
7. -3
8. $=$
9. $>$
10. $<$
BONUS: May

MINUTE 53
1. 80°
2. 1, 2, 3, 6, 9, 18
3. $-\frac{1}{12}$
4. (3, 3)
5. (−3, 2)
6. II
7. Positive
8. 4
9. 1
10. -2
BONUS: 36

MINUTE 54
1. 79°
2. 6
3. 7, 14, 21
4. P(3,−4) G(−5, −4)
5. 8
6. III
7. (7, −4)
8. 2
9. -1
10. 2

MINUTE 55
1. 180°
2. 10
3. 6
4. -7
5. False
6. True
7. $\frac{2}{5}$
8. 9
9. 1
10. -15

MINUTE 56
1. 144
2. -8
3. 11, −1
4. $\begin{bmatrix} 9 \\ -24 \\ 18 \end{bmatrix}$
5. False
6. False
7. $\frac{8}{9}$
8. 2
9. 8
10. 32

MINUTE 57
1. 7
2. ±9
3. −9, 5
4. True
5. $\frac{11}{12}$
6. Yes
7. ±10
8. 2
9. 130
10. -10

MINUTE 58
1. 8
2. ±5
3. 1, −21
4. −13
5. $0.0\overline{38}$
6. $\begin{bmatrix} 5 & 8 \\ 5 & 14 \end{bmatrix}$
7. -3
8. 16
9. ±2
10. 16

MINUTE 59
1. c
2. No
3. 48 sq. units
4. 6.28
5. 2.0707
6. 2.1
7. Degrees in triangle
8. ±9
9. ±8
10. Quadrant III

MINUTE 60
1. b
2. Yes
3. Isosceles
4. d
5. $\frac{4}{3} = 1\frac{1}{3}$
6. c
7. a
8. 8
9. 24
10. $x = 4$

MINUTE ANSWER KEY

MINUTE 61
1. c
2. d
3. a
4. a
5. d
6. 20
7. No
8. $\frac{8}{15}$
9. a
10. c

MINUTE 62
1. a
2. d
3. False
4. True
5. No
6. Parallel
7. d
8. 32
9. 4
10. b

MINUTE 63
1. A
2. D
3. B
4. C
5. 8
6. -2
7. 36
8. $g = b$
9. c
10. b

MINUTE 64
1. C
2. A
3. a
4. b
5. a
6. c
7. 25
8. b
9. c
10. c

MINUTE 65
1. Perpendicular
2. Intersecting
3. Yes
4. 30 in.
5. $10x + 65$
6. $x = 8, y = 4$
7. Acute
8. False
9. a
10. 18

MINUTE 66
1. △
2. Yes
3. Perimeter
4. a
5. c
6. $x = \pm 6$
7. $-12x - 15$
8. Trapezoid
9. 20 cm
10. $x = 11$

MINUTE 67
1. 3
2. c
3. b
4. Acute
5. Right
6. Obtuse
7. ⟷
8. 9
9. 13 in.
10. $-8x + 24$

MINUTE 68
1. d
2. c
3. b
4. True
5. 12.25 ft.²
6. 14 ft.
7. +, •, −
8. ✳
9. c
10. Isosceles

MINUTE 69
1. 14 in.²
2. 5
3. c
4. True
5. b
6. 3.14
7. 7
8. b
9. c
10. a

BONUS: $x = 3$

MINUTE 70
1. D
2. K
3. −1
4. I
5. $5n < 14$
6. False
7. 40
8. 6
9. 6
10. 16

MINUTE 71
1. True
2. d
3. B, D, F, H
4. 75
5. False
6. −2
7. $22b − 33$
8. True
9. $4g^2$
10. 2

BONUS: 8 times larger

MINUTE 72
1. −11
2. False
3. $-7b$
4. negative
5. $710y^3$
6. $\frac{m}{8}, \frac{m}{4}, \frac{m}{3}$
7. >
8. <
9. =
10. >

MINUTE 73
1. $3\frac{1}{4}$, 3.75, $3\frac{4}{5}$
2. $12 − 2x$
3. $y = 16$
4. $2d$
5. 1
6. $24g^3$
7. 9
8. 7
9. (0, 2)
10. (−2, 0)

MINUTE 74
1. 2
2. $10x$
3. b
4. ±4
5. True
6. $y + 5$
7. b
8. d
9. a
10. c

BONUS: 98%

MINUTE 75
1. 9
2. 13
3. $12m + 9$
4. −3
5. 4
6. −18
7. 20
8. 18
9. 20
10. 20

BONUS: 48

MINUTE 76
1. (3 left, 2 up)
2. (2 right, 4 up)
3. 2, 5
4. 27
5. {6}
6. $5a + 15$
7. $9b$
8. $28c$
9. $15b + 10$
10. $-3x$

MINUTE 77
1. $\frac{5}{9}$
2. $\frac{3}{b}$
3. {5}
4. ±7
5. d
6. 20
7. 0
8. d
9. a
10. 10

MINUTE 78
1. $\frac{3}{4t}$
2. $\frac{7}{d}$
3. G
4. $\frac{3s}{8}$
5. $3n + 6 = 9$
6. −10
7. 4
8. d
9. $-24w^3$
10. True

MINUTE 79
1. {5, 7}
2. $-40a^4$
3. c
4. $\frac{3}{4a}$
5. c
6. 6
7. 4
8. 5
9. No
10. No

MINUTE 80
1. True
2. $6a^2 + 7a$
3. Yes
4. True
5. $2b + 4$
6. $20c$
7. 2
8. $4n = 40, n = 10$
9. $n + 4 = 20, n = 16$
10. $\frac{n}{2} = 10, n = 20$

MINUTE ANSWER KEY

MINUTE 81
1. 7 in.
2. $2b + 5$
3. $15g$
4. $30a$
5. $3n + 6 = 12, n = 2$
6. $\frac{4a}{9}$
7. $9a + 4b$
8. -2
9. 2
10. 180

MINUTE 82
1. False
2. b
3. e
4. d
5. c
6. a
7. Yes
8. No
9. $\frac{4}{5}$
10. Positive

MINUTE 83
1. 7
2. 36
3. False
4. $10x$
5. $n > 2$
6. $10y$
7. 62
8. 3
9. 4
10. 100
BONUS: $(1 + 2 + 3 + 6 + 9 + 18 = 39)$

MINUTE 84
1. 28
2. 7
3. 24 ft.^2
4. -8
5. -9
6. $11y - 4x$
7. 4.5
8. 1
9. Quadrant IV
10. $(4, -3)$

MINUTE 85
1. 2
2. 18
3. 12
4. True
5. 12 miles
6. Negative
7. Positive
8. Negative
9. Positive
10. 10, 1, 4

MINUTE 86
1. 1
2. 9
3. 24 ft.^2
4. $8a + 32$
5. 8
6. $2.50
7. $10x$
8. 15
9. $2ab$
10. $\frac{5a}{7}$

MINUTE 87
1. $5a + 15b$
2. $5x^2$
3. $24y^3$
4. 10
5. 4
6. 4
7. 24
8. d
9. 10
10. d

MINUTE 88
1. $\{5, 8\}$
2. 6.5
3. 0.095
4. 10
5. a
6. -4
7. 22
8. 2,000
9. ± 9
10. 2, 8, 12

MINUTE 89
1. 60
2. $\frac{10n}{21y}$
3. $\frac{3a}{4b}$
4. c
5. 6
6. 12
7. $\frac{10ac}{d}$
8. 2 in.
9. a
10. -2

MINUTE 90
1. 16
2. $4x^2 + 12x$
3. $x = 4$
4. 200
5. $3x^2y$
6. $30°$
7. x^7
8. -18
9. -16
10. 9
BONUS: c

MINUTE 91
1. 2
2. $12x - 72$
3. -9
4. -8
5. 6
6. $\frac{a}{b}$
7. $24x^4$
8. -20
9. 1.5 ft.
10. $16y^2$
BONUS: d

MINUTE 92
1. -1
2. 6
3. $-5x + 10$
4. $-x - 6$
5. -7
6. $10x^3$
7. $\frac{a + 2}{c}$
8. True
9. c
10. $(3,0)$

MINUTE 93
1. Yes
2. 5
3. $4x^2 - 24x$
4. 7
5. Yes
6. $a \geq -3$
7. 4
8. 5
9. 2
10. 21

MINUTE 94
1. 7, -7
2. $x \geq 3$
3. $6n + 5n = 33, n = 3$
4. No
5. $x > -1$
6. $5a + 5b + 5c$
7. $y = x + 8$
8. No
9. 3 in.
10. 54 in.^2
BONUS: 28

MINUTE 95
1. 3
2. -8
3. 6
4. $12x^3 - 24x^2 + 6x$
5. 9, -7
6. a
7. 1
8. A line
9. Positive
10. Negative

MINUTE 96
1. No
2. -13
3. 8
4. $\{6, 9, 15\}$
5. a^6
6. $x > -3$
7. b
8. c
9. d
10. a
BONUS: Yes

MINUTE 97
1. $3x + 15$
2. $2x + 16$
3. 2
4. $24x^2 + 48$
5. True
6. False
7. b^2c^3
8. $x > -4.5$
9. 30
10. 80
BONUS: 17 (odd)

MINUTE 98
1. $4x^2 - 8x$
2. $10x - 4$
3. Yes
4. II
5. $(-3, 1)$
6. Positive
7. a
8. b
9. b
10. c

MINUTE 99
1. 3
2. 6
3. Yes
4. No
5. c
6. $\frac{1}{8}$
7. $160°$
8. c
9. a
10. b

MINUTE 100
1. 5
2. 2
3. A
4. ± 20
5. 7
6. $3n = 11$
7. a^7
8. a^6
9. a^2
10. 400 cm^3
BONUS: 3, 17, 21 or 11, 13, 17, or 8, 12, 21